SIX EXPOSURES

Essays in Celebration of the Opening of the

Harrison D. Horblit Collection

of Early Photography

James Blumgarten. *Harrison Horblit*. Reproduced courtesy of Jean Horblit.

SIX EXPOSURES

Essays in Celebration of the Opening of the

Harrison D. Horblit Collection

of Early Photography

THE HOUGHTON LIBRARY

HARVARD UNIVERSITY

1999

I S B N 0-914630-21-0

Library of Congress Catalogue Number 98-075091

TABLE OF CONTENTS

ACKNOWLEDGMENTS

In anticipation of the gift to the Houghton Library of Harrison Horblit's Collection of Early Photography, Houghton colleagues Richard Wendorf, Librarian; Roger Stoddard, Curator of Rare Books and Senior Curator; and Anne Anninger, Philip Hofer Curator of Printing & Graphic Arts convened a planning meeting in November 1995. We invited photography scholars Denise Bethel, Director of Photographs, Sotheby's; Hans P. Kraus, Jr., dealer and publisher in nineteenth-century photographs; Dr. Bates Lowry and Isabel Barrett Lowry, independent scholars; Robin McElheny, Preservation Projects Librarian; and Eugenia Parry, author and Adjunct Professor in the Department of Art and Art History at the University of New Mexico to discuss the future of the Horblit collection at Harvard.

We gratefully acknowledge their expert advice, which established in part the framework for the cataloging, housing, and conservation of the collection. We thank them as well for suggesting the publication of this volume as a way of celebrating the opening of the collection to the general public in March 1999. Such a Festschrift, prepared by Harrison's friends and colleagues most familiar with his photographic interests, is the appropriate tribute to the man and his collection.

The best plans become reality only through hard work. We wish to thank Hans P. Kraus, Jr., Larry J. Schaaf, Grant B. Romer, John Szarkowski, Andrew Szegedy-Maszak, and Robert Sobieszek for their superb contributions. Editor Dorothy Straight met with energy and talent the challenge of knitting together in a coherent whole the work of six gifted and independent essayists. Assistant Curator Julie Mellby's boundless energy and organization kept the project going as she coordinated the work of essayists and editor, photographers and word processor, assisted by Horblit Cataloger Laura Cochrane, and Curatorial Assistant Brenda Breed. To all of them, we are most grateful. So are we to Stephen Sylvester and Robert Zinck of the Photographic Services Department, Harvard College Library, for their meticulous photographic work, and to Duncan Todd and the firm of Champagne/Lafayette Communications Inc. of Natick, Massachusetts, for the elegant design and fine printing of the book itself.

This volume is dedicated to Jean Horblit to express our gratitude for her magnificent gift to the Harvard community and to the students, faculty, and scholars worldwide, whose research, teaching, and publications will be enriched by the collection. Jean's passionate dedication, generosity, and unfailing kindness have earned her the admiration and love of all.

ANNE ANNINGER
Philip Hofer Curator of Printing
& Graphic Arts

WHO IS THE GREATEST OF THEM ALL?
HARRISON D. HORBLIT, HARVARD CLASS OF 1933

Innate curiosity can often lead to the accumulation of facts and sometimes to the mastery of a branch of knowledge. It can also lead to the accumulation of matériel, but seldom to the formation of a collection that resonates like a scientific argument or a work of art. Curiosity when channeled narrowly is just as comprehensible as its results and products, but when it becomes restless, slipping and sliding about, it baffles and confounds us by its effects. Harrison Horblit (1912–1988) was one of the great collectors of his day, but much as we admire the integrity of his character, laud his explorations in various fields, and pay tribute to his collections, we will not be able to explain what it is that he was doing. There was just too much restless curiosity there for us to deal with.

Reading up, particularly inside the academy, is the usual antidote for curiosity, but some subjects cannot be handled that way. Harrison's friend David Wheatland discovered that his curiosity about the experimental and demonstrational instruments of science, including pocket dials, exceeded the scanty literature on the subject, so he collected the books and pamphlets both printed and illustrated as well as the instruments, illustrated or not. His Collection of Historical Scientific Instruments now makes possible at Harvard the construction of the books and articles which he yearned for in his youth. (Thank goodness the literature didn't exist then, or he would have been denied a great deal of fun and excitement over a long collecting career.)

Harrison began by collecting Science. At best Photography was his third subject. More likely it was his fourth or fifth after Science, but Photography, after all, is an experimental, scientific, and revolutionary subject. He admitted debts to Professor L. J. Henderson whose undergraduate course "instilled" in him "the urge to collect works in the History of Science" and to the Houghton Librarian William A. Jackson, whose complete dedication to Harvard was a match for his own. There was his yachtsman's sentiment for the literature of navigation. Only eight years ago his widow, Jean, discovered in a cupboard and gave to the Library a handful of his eighteenth-century longitude tracts, most of which were not at Harvard and at least one of which was unrecorded.

The Science collection was validated in 1958 when Harrison mounted at the Grolier Club his celebrated exhibition of "One Hundred Books Famous in Science." Eight years later the four-hundred-and-fifty-page catalogue was published, clinching Harrison's international reputation as scholar-collector. Already in 1958 Harrison was collecting material on Sir Thomas Phillipps, the greatest of all book collectors, and he mounted a Grolier Club exhibition on him in 1972. In 1994 Jean Horblit gave that collection to the Club, where it occupies a room specially outfitted for it, and which published a catalogue in 1997.

From the middle 1940s Harrison was presenting books to Houghton Library. Over the years predictable subjects included navigation, arithmetic, general science, and early photography, but there were also book catalogues and printer's manuals, bookbindings and early English printing, and some great early manuscripts. Included were forty-one fifteenth-century books! There was the ninth-century Jerome[1] from the abbey of Saint Maximinus at Trier, the oldest substantial manuscript at Harvard. No wonder that such a staunch library supporter was appointed to the Overseers' Committee to Visit the University Library and served as Honorary Curator of the History of Science from 1963.

Harrison was fully capable of behaving like a librarian from time to time. After his retirement he and his wife, Jean, moved to a palatial pond-side villa in Ridgefield, Connecticut. He noticed at auction in 1973 a unique Revolutionary War print of the Battle of Ridgefield, and when the funds he raised locally proved insufficient he expended his own, declaring that the print belonged in the town. It hangs there today in Keeler Tavern. But just for Harrison, one Harvard librarian created the formulation "Kepler is the Milton of Science." Harvard, you see, has one of the three great Milton collections, and it has the greatest Kepler collection in the Americas, but one that requires keeping up. When Harrison was solicited for funds to buy an exceedingly rare Kepler, he telephoned back: "R-r-roger, I'm not going to give you the money."

But when a Houghton librarian and a History of Science professor spent a night in Ridgefield in the usual sumptuous Jean-and-Harrison hospitality, only a few words were sufficient to elicit the gift of Tycho Brahe's *De Nova . . . Stella* (Copenhagen, 1573), needed for an imminent exhibition on Danish Literature. At a celebration of the exhibition the great Danish bibliopole Hans Bagger declared that the Tycho was the only irreplaceable item in the room.

---

1. In 1956 Harrison bought from H. P. Kraus, offered separately priced for sale, two ninth-century manuscripts from Trier, the Jerome now at Harvard and a Bede—"one of the most famous and most significant Carolingian scientific manuscripts," it has been called. On a Sunday in 1979 three Houghton librarians drove from Cambridge to Ridgefield through the rainiest of dark days to lunch with the Horblits and view collections. They complimented Harrison for keeping the two Trier manuscripts together, and they begged him to place the Bede beside the Jerome at Harvard. Before the week was out, Harrison tested the earnest of his library friends by selling back the manuscript to Kraus.

ROGER E. STODDARD

In 1983 Houghton Library mounted an exhibition in celebration of Harrison's fiftieth Harvard reunion, receiving Harrison's classmates at an opening on Commencement afternoon. Professor Owen Gingerich organized the books and manuscripts and wrote the catalogue, *Collector's Choice*. Printed by the Stinehour Press and designed by Stephen Harvard, it pleased one and all; it must have surprised many readers to learn about Harrison's extensive and magnificent gifts to Harvard. The book world thought that he had sold all his science—at least by authors whose names began with letters A through G—in two 1974 Sotheby auctions. In 1984 Harrison endowed a book-acquisition fund for antiquarian books about books, book catalogues, and bibliography. Harrison knew firsthand the necessity of such tools. Then, in 1990, Jean Horblit established the Harrison D. Horblit Fund for the History of Science, the first Houghton Library acquisition fund endowed for that important branch of the collections.

And the photographs? In 1961 Harrison had purchased from the London bookdealers Lionel and Philip Robinson the pioneer photographs and negatives collected by Sir Thomas Phillipps. His immediate grasp of the importance of the subject and the allure of his holding drew him into the new collecting field, and he persevered with full ardor. By 1974 when the Grolier Club mounted its exhibition of books illustrated with photographs —"The Truthful Lens"—Harrison could lend from his growing collection; and his copies provided many of the illustrations in the catalogue published in 1980. As Harvard began to plan its celebration that came to be called "The Invention of Photography and its Impact on Learning," Harrison detected a validation of his new hobby at the old school, but he did not live to see the many exhibitions mounted in Cambridge in November 1989 or the extensive illustrated collection of essays that they inspired. His widow, Jean, supported the project with a very generous gift. His own photographs, selected and arranged by his friend Eugenia Janis, were shown in the Houghton cases and recorded in a separate catalogue.

In 1997 Jean Horblit gave Harrison's trove of 6,500 photographic items to Harvard: the largest collection of daguerreotypes (3,141), the largest collection of paper negatives (360), 1,700 albumen silver prints, 1,000 salted paper prints, 370 books and albums illustrated with photographs, 105 ambrotypes, and much else. Just as Harvard has important and representative holdings of all the prior graphic processes (woodcut, printed book, engraving, and lithograph), now Harvard can offer a study and research collection on Photography to its scholars and students. Houghton Library has expanded its resources in a systematic and elegant development, so that it will make new contributions to the work of the University.

Several months ago Houghton's librarians spotted a Hallotype from 1857, an exceedingly rare cased double paper print, varnished and colored. Harrison didn't have one, so it has been purchased for Harvard. As we admired it in the Graphic Arts study room, I thought I could just hear from the near corner, "B-b-but, Roger . . . "

Harrison Horblit stands as an inspiration to others, the archetype of the great collector, accomplished but unpredictable, self-assured but inexplicable. What do you suppose he would be collecting now? Follow your curiosity, he might say, find out what's important, and get it. Take your own advice, never mind what others do or say, expect neither sympathy nor understanding—unless, perhaps, you are doing it for Harvard!

ROGER E. STODDARD
Curator of Rare Books
in the Harvard College Library

F IGURE 1.   Beard Studio. *Sir Thomas Phillipps*, ca. 1842. Ninth plate daguerreotype, in a sixth plate Wharton case. Reproduced courtesy of The Grolier Club.

"What Would I Want with Photography?
I'm Collecting History of Science!"
Recalling Harrison Horblit

Hans P. Kraus, Jr.

Harrison Horblit[1] (frontispiece) once remarked to me that his interest in photography paralleled the first three decades of *my* life. By the end of that span, thanks in great measure to his example and inspiration, I, too, had become devoted to the study of this fascinating medium. Jean and Harrison Horblit, friends of my parents, in later years enjoyed telling the story of how my father had jubilantly distributed cigars in celebration of my birth at the reception for The Grolier Club's seminal 1958 exhibition "One Hundred Books Famous in Science," which Horblit curated. Around the same time, Horblit later told me, he had purchased, sight unseen, the photography collection of the great book and manuscript collector Sir Thomas Phillipps[2] (figure 1). It was his earlier interest in collecting books on the history of science, together with his ardent fascination with Sir Thomas Phillipps, that would gradually persuade Horblit to shift his focus from book collecting to collecting photography.

Shortly after graduating from Harvard, Horblit inaugurated what would eventually become his celebrated collection of the history of science. His first acquisitions were books on the subject of navigation, reflecting his early passion for yachting; from there, he proceeded to study and collect works on all aspects of the history of science, from astronomy to zoology. It was inevitable that photography titles should be included. His important exhibition catalogue, *One Hundred Books Famous in Science*,[3] still one of the standard references in the field, contains three entries relating to photography.[4] Horblit's comment in an entry on a book by Daguerre notes, "The beginnings of photography, a major tool in science."[5] If Horblit had revised this catalogue after undertaking the study of his own photographic holdings, I believe he would have included two titles by Henry Fox Talbot: *The Pencil of Nature* (figure 2), the first photographically illustrated book,[6] which Talbot used to promote the process he had invented; and *Some Account of the Art of Photogenic Drawing, or The Process by Which Natural Objects May Be Made to Delineate Themselves without the Aid of the Artist's Pencil*,[7] an offprint that constitutes the first separate publication ever on the subject of photography.

Jean Horblit's recollections of the acquisition of the Phillipps photography collection are revealing. She remembers a phone call from the Robinson brothers at some point before August 1961, offering the collection for sale, and her husband's initial response: "Now, what would I want with photography? I'm collecting history of science!" Some time later, however, Harrison turned to his wife and exclaimed, "What am I saying? Photography is *part* of science!" He called the Robinson brothers back directly and instructed, "Send it!" Jean recalls the day the huge crate arrived, filled with photography of every kind: daguerreotypes, calotypes, salt and albumen prints, and photographically illustrated books. Harrison had the time of his life unpacking it, she says.

Despite his obvious pleasure at owning Sir Thomas's photographs, it was not until the 1970s that Horblit gave his photographic holdings his full attention and started actively adding to that nucleus. He lent several books for "The Truthful Lens," the landmark 1974 exhibition of photographically illustrated books curated by Lucien Goldschmidt and Weston Naef at The Grolier Club. It was almost certainly in connection with this event that he first met Sam Wagstaff, a fellow lender to the exhibition, who was to influence and encourage him in his approach to photography. Wagstaff had been curator of paintings at the Wadsworth Athenaeum and then at the Detroit Institute of Art before retiring from museum work to devote himself to private collecting. One of the great collectors and tastemakers in the soon-to-be-burgeoning field of nineteenth- and early twentieth-century photographs,[8] Wagstaff had a particular interest in the seascapes by Gustave Le Gray that Horblit owned. Jean Horblit can remember Wagstaff's pleading with her husband to tell him first if he ever decided to sell them. This sort of enthusiasm on the part of a passionate connoisseur is just the encouragement an acquisitive person needs to stimulate his or her own collecting instinct, and so it was for Harrison Horblit, who soon began to buy photographs much more actively. Not competing with Wagstaff's catholic approach, Horblit instead focused his efforts on the earliest years of photography, collecting whatever was available on paper or on metal. By the time the catalogue for "The Truthful Lens"[9] was finally published, in 1980, Horblit had managed to acquire many more of the books that had appeared in the exhibition six years before, and freely supplied the catalogue illustrations.

Although my parents had long known the Horblits through the rare-book world, I believe it was my father's and Harrison's shared fascination with Sir Thomas Phillipps that was the true catalyst for their lifelong friendship.[10] Sir Thomas, it seems, left a legacy not only of collections, but also of inspiration for future generations of collectors.

A renowned bibliomaniac, Sir Thomas Phillipps[11] lived from 1792 to 1872 and during his lifetime amassed one of the greatest libraries ever, comprising more than sixty

FIGURE 2.   William Henry Fox Talbot. Title page of *The Pencil of Nature* (London: Longman, Brown, Green and Longmans, 1844–46); volume: 30.5 x 24.4 cm.

thousand manuscripts and over forty thousand printed books. He would buy any kind of manuscript at all on papyrus, vellum, or paper, including deeds, charters, and pedigrees, but the universality of his collecting vision did not let him stop there: he wrote in 1869, "I am buying Printed Books because I wish to have *one Copy of every Book in the World!!!!!*"[12]

My father and Horblit, it seems, indulged in a sort of hero worship: their common desire to possess anything collected, printed, or even touched by Sir Thomas came close to reproducing Sir Thomas's own preoccupation. Luckily, however, neither my father nor Horblit took his collecting zeal to the ruthless extremes for which Sir Thomas himself was famous. Single-minded to the point of obsession, Phillipps nearly ruined his family through his neglect. Over the years, his library overtook his country manor: Lady Phillipps portrayed herself as having been "booked out of one wing [of the house] and ratted out of the other."[13] It was out of this vast accumulation that Harrison Horblit's trove of photography came in 1961. And it was into that trove that I had the good fortune of wandering as an impressionable young man.

Toward the end of my teens, in the 1970s, my childhood aspiration to become a photographer matured into an interest in the history of photography. My parents often took me along on their visits to the Horblits, where Harrison patiently nurtured my curiosity. While the four of them played bridge, I was allowed to explore the photography library, at that time still housed in the Phillipps Room, Harrison's private study above the main entrance. The wonders I discovered in that room during those first forays were to form the foundation for the lessons Horblit would teach me about photography and collecting over the ensuing years.

Among the photographic incunabula from Sir Thomas's hoard, I remember finding the two most important books by Henry Fox Talbot: a complete presentation copy of *The Pencil of Nature* (which Horblit informed me was rarer than my father's Gutenberg Bible)[14] and a copy of *Sun Pictures in Scotland,*[15] which, in following the footsteps of Sir Walter Scott, represented the very first use of photography as a travel guide. In both of these books, the plates were uneven in color and mostly quite pale, traits that I later learned were characteristic of every publication containing Talbot's photographs. Horblit felt that given the difficulties Talbot had experienced in preserving his images, it was remarkable that so many had survived at all, and he was always strangely attracted to these pale images, perhaps fascinated by their very precariousness and fragility. He must be credited with preserving for us a number of historically important examples of early photography that other collectors did not know how to value.

I particularly recall being dazzled by a group of pink, violet, and yellow photogenic drawings by Talbot. As I stared at them, the colors seemed to be changing before my eyes

—and I am afraid that what we now know about these most light-sensitive of all photographs suggests that they probably were! Especially vivid, even now, is my memory of a study in deep lavender of a pair of fallen leaves (figure 3). Its bold simplicity I found stunning, and the realization that the image had been made by photography's inventor filled me with wonder.

Harrison Horblit would soon begin to add yet more works by Talbot to the original Phillipps collection. His ability to recognize value in even the faded images guided his approach to collecting the work of Talbot and his circle. He started to buy individual Talbotypes, as Talbot's salt prints were termed in their day, preferring prints that were mounted; he didn't mind if they had turned a pale brown or green, since that was, after all, how they appeared in Talbot's various publications.[16] A few richly toned, less faded, and untrimmed prints were also available on the market at the time, but Horblit did not confine himself to these more obviously desirable examples. He helped me to understand the value of relics dating from the beginnings of photography—and especially those that evidenced the passage of time—as irreplaceable original documents, displaying the imperfections that so frequently occurred in the early years of this infant process.

FIGURE 3. William Henry Fox Talbot. *A Pair of Leaves*, watermarked 1839. Photogenic drawing negative; image: 11.4 x 18.9 cm.

Another memory of my afternoons in Horblit's library concerns some curious albums of calotype negatives and salt prints, including still-lives of manuscripts and artifacts arranged on drawing-room furniture. When I inquired about them, I was told that they were the work from the 1850s of a Mrs. Guppy. Today, having seen much more nineteenth-century photography in the interim, I am more intrigued than ever by this mysterious body of work. Surprisingly little has been known about Mrs. Guppy until recently, when Larry Schaaf began doing research for his fascinating essay, which follows this one in the present volume.

One day I discovered in the Phillipps collection a group of large salt prints of Egypt by Félix Teynard, which conveyed the mystery of that ancient land better than any other images I have seen. In one of these, *Égypte: Karnak (Thèbes), Troisième Pylône—Colosse de Spath Calcaire en D, pl. 65* (figure 4), the pharaoh's lifelike torso seems almost ready to break out of its limestone confines. These examples inspired my own hunt for Teynard, eventually leading to my finding, in Paris, a complete copy of his magnificent *Égypte et Nubie*, which served as the source for the *Catalogue Raisonné*.[17]

The collection's three proto-Impressionist seascapes by Gustave Le Gray also seemed to me truly sublime. *The Brig upon the Water* (figure 5), with its mussel beds in the foreground, the masts of the brig gently piercing the horizon, and storm clouds massing overhead, bears witness to the photographer's early training as a painter. Not only the artistic effects but, even more, the technical achievement involved in capturing such dramatic clouds had excited the wonder and envy of Le Gray's contemporaries. The picture caused a sensation at the London Photographic Society's 1856 exhibition, where it was heralded as the "grandest effort ever seen in photography."[18]

The few daguerreotypes in the original Phillipps trove inspired an ancillary obsession for Horblit, whose own collection ultimately grew to comprise about 3,200 examples, an impressive quantity by any standard. I remember seeing some tarnished daguerreotypes about which Harrison ironically remarked, "You wouldn't show these to your mother-in-law." Daguerreotypes are generally collected in categories, whether by photographer, location, subject, or type—famous people, occupationals, people with pets, hand-colored, and so on—but Horblit felt constrained by no such considerations. His goal was simply to collect as many daguerreotypes as possible and then sort them by size; he would buy whatever he could find within his price range, and the bigger the better. Driven by much the same instinct for preservation that had once led Sir Thomas Phillipps to acquire even ordinary deeds just to save them from certain destruction, Horblit knew that these precious, unique, vernacular portraits, then neglected by collectors, could be easily scattered or lost if he did not snatch them up. He thus amassed a gallery of mid-nineteenth-century

FIGURE 4.   Felix Teynard. *Égypte: Karnak (Thèbes), Troisième Pylône—Colosse de Spath Calcaire, en D* from *Égypte et Nubie* (Paris: Goupil et Cie, 1858), pl. 65. Salted paper print; image: 26 x 30.4 cm., mount: 42.1 x 52.3 cm.

American faces, some identified, some bearing place-names, but most anonymous. Were they graduates? Newlyweds? Captains of industry? Post-mortems? Such questions about our unnamed forebears, and their untold stories, intrigued him. I think he would be pleased to know that his daguerreotype collection, with its mysterious faces, will be preserved for future generations to contemplate.

The inspiration of those early hours spent in Horblit's Phillipps Room will remain with me forever, but that experience represented only the beginning of the influence Horblit himself was to have on my career. At just the right moment, he encouraged me to take my interests out into the world. My first independent exposure to the specialist world of photography came in 1978, when Harrison encouraged me to attend a collectors' sym-

FIGURE 5. Gustave Le Gray. *The Brig upon the Water*, 1856. Albumen silver print; image: 31.5 x 41 cm., mount: 53.5 x 66.3 cm.

posium, auction, and trade fair at the George Eastman House in Rochester. This was an important occasion for me: I met curators, collectors, and dealers and saw wonderful photographs from all periods; there was an almost palpable energy and excitement in the air. As it turned out, it was this event that inspired the formation of the Association of International Photography Art Dealers.[19]

After college, I was employed in the Photographs Department at Christie's, first in London and then in New York, cataloguing large quantities of material ranging from photogenic drawings, daguerreotypes, photographically illustrated books, and albums to twentieth-century prints, both vintage and later. Thus immersed in the auction world, I began to gain some sophistication about the commercial realities of the art market and

HANS P. KRAUS, JR.

who the players were. I was astonished by the relatively low prices commanded by the work of such pioneers as Talbot, especially in contrast to the values placed on work by more modern photographers. Moreover, some of the Talbot prints were not as faded as those owned by Harrison Horblit. I could feel myself starting to think like a dealer.

In England, I was able to study the Talbot collections at the Science Museum, the Fox Talbot Museum, and the Royal Photographic Society, which opened my eyes to the diversity and true art of William Henry Fox Talbot and his circle. My newfound expertise gave me greater confidence in my own independent judgment about the work of these British pioneers, and in turn helped me to evaluate what I saw at the salesrooms. One auction was of particular importance: the sale of the collection of Nevil Story-Maskelyne and his wife, born Theresa Dillwyn Llewelyn, an untouched source fresh out of a fabled British country house. I helped to research and catalogue this material, which included many examples by Talbot, John Dillwyn Llewelyn, and Story-Maskelyne himself, an important pioneer whose work had never before been available on the market. I remember my excitement in describing these treasures to Horblit over the phone. It was probably obvious to him before it was to me that photography was to be my vocation, but like a true mentor, he bided his time and allowed me to arrive at this conclusion on my own.

My father had always wanted me to work in his bookshop, which specialized in illuminated manuscripts and early printed books. In the end I chose not to enter the family firm but instead to start my own business dealing in early photographs and photographically illustrated books. This decision may not seem such a great departure now, but at the time it felt colossal. Only the fact that his friend Harrison Horblit was so interested in— indeed, nearly consumed by—photography made the field almost acceptable to my father. Horblit was an elder who respected me, I believe, as much for my independence as for my choice of specialization, and that respect provided me with some much-needed moral support.

In December 1983, after three and a half years spent at Christie's in London and New York, I went into business for myself, as a private dealer. My own collection, begun six years earlier, became my inventory and Harrison Horblit my first serious client. On weekend visits to my parents' house in Ridgefield, Connecticut, I would bring along items to show him. Dealing with such a seasoned and shrewd collector taught me a lot about the financial side of the business. Afterward I would report to my father what I had sold and how much profit I had made, trying hard to impress him. My initial success with Horblit lent me the confidence to begin offering photographs to others. London auctions were still held three times a year, and Horblit routinely commissioned me to bid for him on significant items. I followed my father's advice and always reserved the right to bid beyond a client's limit on my own behalf, agreeing to offer the client first refusal; on those occasions when I exceeded his limit, Horblit invariably ended up buying the lot anyway.

On one item he gave me a huge limit. In 1984 a copy of *Record of the Death-Bed of C.M.W.* (figure 6) came up at Christie's in London, estimated at £1,000 to £1,500. Illustrated with a photographic frontispiece and produced during the same period as the first fascicle of *The Pencil of Nature*, the book had been printed by Talbot's former assistant, Nicolaas Henneman, in a very small quantity and only for private distribution.[20] Horblit did not own it and gave me an order to bid up to £20,000. I got it for a mere £2,200! At the same auction I also successfully secured for him the Stewart family copy of *The Pencil of Nature* for £30,000.

I learned an important lesson from Horblit as a result of this transaction. The evening after I successfully executed the order bids on his behalf for a total of £32,200, I telephoned him to report his victories. He was pleased, and so was I: I intended to use the 10 percent bidding commission I would be receiving to help finance inventory purchases during my continued European travels. On my return to New York, I called Horblit again to brief him in greater detail about the auction the previous week. He said, "I assume you have covered yourself. Have you seen today's exchange rate for the pound?" Since I had a thirty-day credit account at the auction house, I was not obliged to pay immediately, but in the week subsequent to the sale, the British pound had risen 9 percent against the dollar. Horblit then told me about banking contracts for currency futures, commonly used in business to protect against the gamble of monetary fluctuations. I thanked him and assured him that I would use such a device the next time. He replied, "I expect you will, because I plan to pay you at the exchange rate in effect on the auction date." This meant that my commission was no longer 10 percent but rather 1 percent. There was no discussion—just a lesson never to be forgotten.

Horblit often preached the importance of providing proper descriptions for items being offered for sale, and complained that most photography dealers' standards fell far short of his own in this regard. Coming as he did from the rare-book world, he could never find enough catalogues to keep him busy. He yearned for accurate descriptive and provenance information and was as pleased when he found it as he was enraged when he didn't. Given his high standards, I felt proud to learn of his satisfaction with my series of Sun Pictures catalogues, and even more so when I saw him annotating and referring to them.

Harrison Horblit brought to his teaching an enthusiasm generated by his own continuing research. He would frequently explore new ideas in ongoing dialogue with me, or

FIGURE 6.   Nicolaas Henneman. *Bust of Catherine Mary Walter*, frontispiece and title page of [John Walter], *Record of the Death-Bed of C.M.W.* (London: Gilbert & Rivington, 1844). Salted paper print; image: 8.2 x 6.8 cm.; volume: 14.9 x 9.7 cm.

test me in order to test himself. Bibliographical questions and inconsistencies would hound him until he could come up with some logical (if often complicated) solution. His experience in this area was invaluable to Larry Schaaf and me as we began our *Pencil of Nature* research in the mid-1980s. Harrison and Jean Horblit provided endless encouragement and unlimited access to their extensive Talbot holdings. Horblit possessed more copies of this book than had anyone else since the inventor himself. One he gave to the

Pierpont Morgan Library; another—the Stewart family copy—was presented by Jean in Harrison's memory to The Metropolitan Museum of Art; a third was sold; parts 1 and 2 of yet another copy were donated to the Houghton Library during Horblit's lifetime; and one complete and one partial copy, as well as numerous individual plates, have now also come to Houghton as part of the Horblit collection. Using all of these, he helped us to identify variant plates that might otherwise have gone undetected. He also taught us the principles of "sophistication"—that is, as applied here, the methodology of filling out an incomplete book with authentic components from elsewhere. In January 1989, my firm published H. Fox Talbot's *The Pencil of Nature Anniversary Facsimile* in commemoration of the 150th anniversary of Talbot's invention. I deeply regret that Harrison Horblit did not live to see the completed publication; he had died just ten months earlier.

By the end of his life, Harrison Horblit had completed his metamorphosis from book collector to photography collector. He ennobled the field by bringing his seriousness of purpose to its pursuit. A true Harvard man, Horblit would be overjoyed to know that his collection of photography now resides permanently in the Houghton Library. For my part, I am glad that his legacy of inspiration will be passed down to future generations. Jean Horblit's generous gift to Harvard in her husband's memory has made possible the University's new commitment to photographic discovery.

HANS P. KRAUS, JR.

NOTES

1. For a biographical sketch, see G. Thomas Tanselle, "Harrison D. Horblit, Collector," *Gazette of The Grolier Club*, new ser. 48 (New York: The Grolier Club, 1997): 5–17.

2. Although Horblit had been offered this collection somewhat earlier by the London bookseller Lionel and Philip Robinson, he did not finally purchase it until 1961. This was after he had already bought from them the bulk of his Phillippsiana. See Eric Holzenberg, *The Middle Hill Press: A Checklist of the Horblit Collection of Books, Tracts, Leaflets, and Broadsides Printed by Sir Thomas Phillipps at His Press at Middle Hill, or Elsewhere to His Order, Now in the Library of The Grolier Club* (New York: The Grolier Club, 1997).

3. Harrison Horblit, *One Hundred Books Famous in Science* (New York: The Grolier Club, 1964).

4. The three entries are as follows: no. 21a. Louis Jacques Mandé Daguerre, *Historique et Description des procédés du Daguerréotype* (Paris: Lerebours-Susse Frères, 1839); no. 21b. Francois Arago, *Rapport . . . sur le Daguerréotype* (Paris: Bachelier, 1839); no. 90. Wilhelm Conrad Röntgen, *Ueber eine neue Art von Strahlen . . .*, 2 parts (Würzburg: Stahel, 1896–97).

5. Horblit, no. 21a, Daguerre.

6. H. Fox Talbot, *The Pencil of Nature* (London: Longman, Brown, Green and Longmans, 1844). The 150th anniversary limited-edition facsimile (New York: Hans P. Kraus, Jr., Inc., 1989) includes an introductory volume by Larry J. Schaaf containing reviews by contemporary critics, an analysis of each plate and its variants, and a census of surviving copies.

7. Henry Fox Talbot, *Some Account of the Art of Photogenic Drawing, or The Process by Which Natural Objects May Be Made to Delineate Themselves Without the Aid of the Artist's Pencil* (London: R. and J. E. Edwards, 1839).

8. Horblit proposed Wagstaff for membership in The Grolier Club; he was elected in 1977.

9. Lucien Goldschmidt and Weston J. Naef, *The Truthful Lens: A Survey of the Photographically Illustrated Book, 1844–1914* (New York: The Grolier Club, 1980).

10. See H. P. Kraus, *A Rare Book Saga* (New York: G. P. Putnam's Sons, 1978), 223–26.

11. See A. N. L. Munby, *Portrait of an Obsession: The Life of Sir Thomas Phillipps, the World's Greatest Book Collector* (London: Constable, 1967), adapted by Nicolas Barker from the five volumes of *Phillipps Studies*.

12. A. N. L. Munby, *The Formation of the Phillipps Library from 1841 to 1872*, Phillipps Studies No. 4 (Cambridge: Cambridge University Press, 1956), 139.

13. A. N. L. Munby, *The Family Affairs of Sir Thomas Phillipps*, Phillipps Studies No. 2 (Cambridge: Cambridge University Press, 1952), 91.

14. According to the most recently published version of Larry Schaaf's census, begun in the introductory volume to *The Pencil of Nature* facsimile, thirty-nine virtually complete copies survive, eleven of which are preserved in the original six fascicles with wrappers. See Larry J. Schaaf, "Henry Fox Talbot's *The Pencil of Nature*: A Revised Census of Original Copies," *History of Photography* 17, no. 4 (1993): 388–96.

15. H. Fox Talbot, *Sun Pictures in Scotland* (London: Longman, Brown, Green and Longmans, 1845).

16. There are a number of possible reasons for the varying degrees of fading evident in these published prints, among them impure chemicals, contaminated water, insufficient washing, glues used for mounting, atmospheric pollutants, and wide fluctuations in storage humidity and temperature, not to mention damage caused by Talbot's own attempts to stabilize his prints, which were already recorded as losing color during his lifetime. For a discussion on the fading of Talbot's prints, see Larry J. Schaaf's introductory volume to the anniversary facsimile of *The Pencil of Nature*, 38–43.

17. Felix Teynard, *Calotypes of Egypt—A Catalogue Raisonné*, with essay by Kathleen Stewart Howe (New York, London, and Carmel, Calif.: Hans P. Kraus, Jr., Inc., Robert Hershkowitz Ltd., and Weston Gallery, Inc., 1992).

18. Helmut Gernsheim, *The History of Photography from the Earliest Use of the Camera Obscura in the Eleventh Century up to 1914* (London: Oxford University Press, 1955), 199. For a more extensive discussion on Le Gray, see Eugenia Parry Janis, *The Photography of Gustave Le Gray* (Chicago: The Art Institute of Chicago, 1987).

19. Ever since, AIPAD has been sponsoring the most important annual trade fair for nineteenth- and twentieth-century photography.

20. Schaaf, *The Pencil of Nature*, introductory volume, 85, n. 8.

"Splendid Calotypes"
Henry Talbot, Amelia Guppy,
Sir Thomas Phillipps,
and Photographs on Paper

Larry J. Schaaf

On entering Sir Thomas Phillipps's house at Middle Hill in 1845, Lady Pauline Trevelyan found it

> piled [from] floor to ceiling right & left with books in cases & out of cases & in boxes & packages—the walls of the stair case the same. The passage at the top is in the same plight, with the addition of a bookcase down the middle. The principal room is so full of MSS that only a thin person can wriggle themselves along the passages left between the solid walls of paper. The dining room is deluged. Drawing room and billiard room given over to the books.

A correspondent of Ruskin, Pauline visited Phillipps with her husband, Sir Walter Calverley Trevelyan, a childhood friend of William Henry Fox Talbot. She recorded their welcome at Middle Hill:

> the dining room table & some chairs were cleared today in honour of our arrival—at considerable trouble I fear. They received us very kindly and showed us many most beautiful and curious books. Lovely MSS with illuminations—Gospels, old histories & classics—Virgil . . . illuminated MSS seem quite common things here.

Yet amid so many ancient volumes of "such exuberance of riches in that way I never saw or imagined," a very modern book stood out in Pauline Trevelyan's memory: Sir Thomas "showed me a Number of Talbots Pencil of Nature. Splendid calotypes."[1]

"Splendid calotypes"! Although less than five years old at the time of this visit, William Henry Fox Talbot's invention of a practical photographic process on paper was already beginning to assert itself among the more traditional methods of printing and reproduction. Talbot had expressed the hope that his process would make "every man his own printer & publisher" and enable "authors to make facsimiles of their works in their own handwriting;" for Sir Thomas, photography's potential precisely to copy his manuscripts and to create other forms of facsimile was irresistible.[2]

If Harrison Horblit's Connecticut home was not nearly so densely packed as had been Middle Hill, it had nonetheless absorbed a goodly part of the latter's riches. And in impulsively acquiring Sir Thomas's collection of photography, Harrison Horblit had likewise absorbed much of his hero's fascination with the youthful medium. I still remember my first visit to Horblit's house. In short order I was holding Sir Thomas's copy of *The Pencil of Nature*, likely the very one that had so impressed Lady Trevelyan a century and a half before. The occasion was to lay the groundwork for what would become the limited edition 1989 *Anniversary Facsimile* of Talbot's seminal publication.[3] The eclectic nature of Horblit's collection, shaped in no small way by the voracious appetite of Sir Thomas Phillipps himself, was critical to elucidating the structure of Talbot's pioneering work. Harrison Horblit's own detailed knowledge, both of his own collection and of book practices generally, led to some challenging questions. His enthusiasm was an important underpinning for the project in its earliest days. I only regret that he never saw the final product, one greatly influenced by the early role he played in shaping its form.

William Henry Fox Talbot's invention of photography was in fact the result of an embarrassing deficiency. A man of attainments in many fields, and a member of the Reform Parliament, he was entering the prime of his professional and personal life by the 1830s.[4] He married during Parliament's Christmas break in 1832, and in the course of the following summer began touring the continent with his new wife, Constance. By autumn, they found themselves on the Italian shores of Lake Como, where they met up with Talbot's half-sister Caroline and other family members. In October 1833, at Villa Melzi outside the village of Bellagio, Talbot's manifold skills failed him: everyone around him was happily sketching away, but Talbot himself could not draw. Turning to science, he attempted once again to employ the aid of the *camera lucida*, a prismatic aid for draughtsmen, which imparted a verisimilitude that was of great value to scientists (and, it must be said, to more artists than was generally admitted). Despite the realistic image offered by the camera, Talbot unfortunately still lacked the visual skills of the draughtsman. The image presented to his eye by the camera did little to help him reduce the complex and colorful three-dimensional world to pencil lines on paper.[5] As Talbot himself later recalled in the introduction to *The Pencil of Nature*, his camera drawings were "melancholy to behold." But he was a man of science, and it was to science that he turned for help. Realizing that the optical image produced in a related instrument, the *camera obscura*, was nothing more than a succession of stronger and weaker areas of light, Talbot wondered if he might employ the well-known powers of sunlight to affect a coating on a sheet of paper placed in the camera.

FIGURE 7. William Henry Fox Talbot. *Sharington's Tower, Lacock Abbey, from the Southeast*, September 23 [1839?] Photogenic drawing negative; image: 9.1 x 9.8 cm.

Thus was the idea of photography born. Talbot could do nothing to put it into effect while traveling, and then on his return to England faced demanding Parliamentary and mathematical duties. Sometime during the spring of 1834, however, as the sunlight began to regain its power, he began his experiments. Although he did not consider chemistry to be his strong point, Talbot was highly educated and possessed of a good library at Lacock Abbey. His previous readings led him to investigate the light-sensitive properties of silver chloride. By soaking writing paper in a solution of common table salt, drying it, and then flowing over it a coating of silver nitrate, he set up a chemical reaction, entrapping the resultant light-sensitive silver chloride within the fibers of the paper. Once dry, this paper could be positioned under an opaque object (such as a leaf or a feather) and exposed to the sun. The silver chloride was reduced to metallic silver wherever the light struck, creating a colored image. Where the object blocked the light, the paper remained

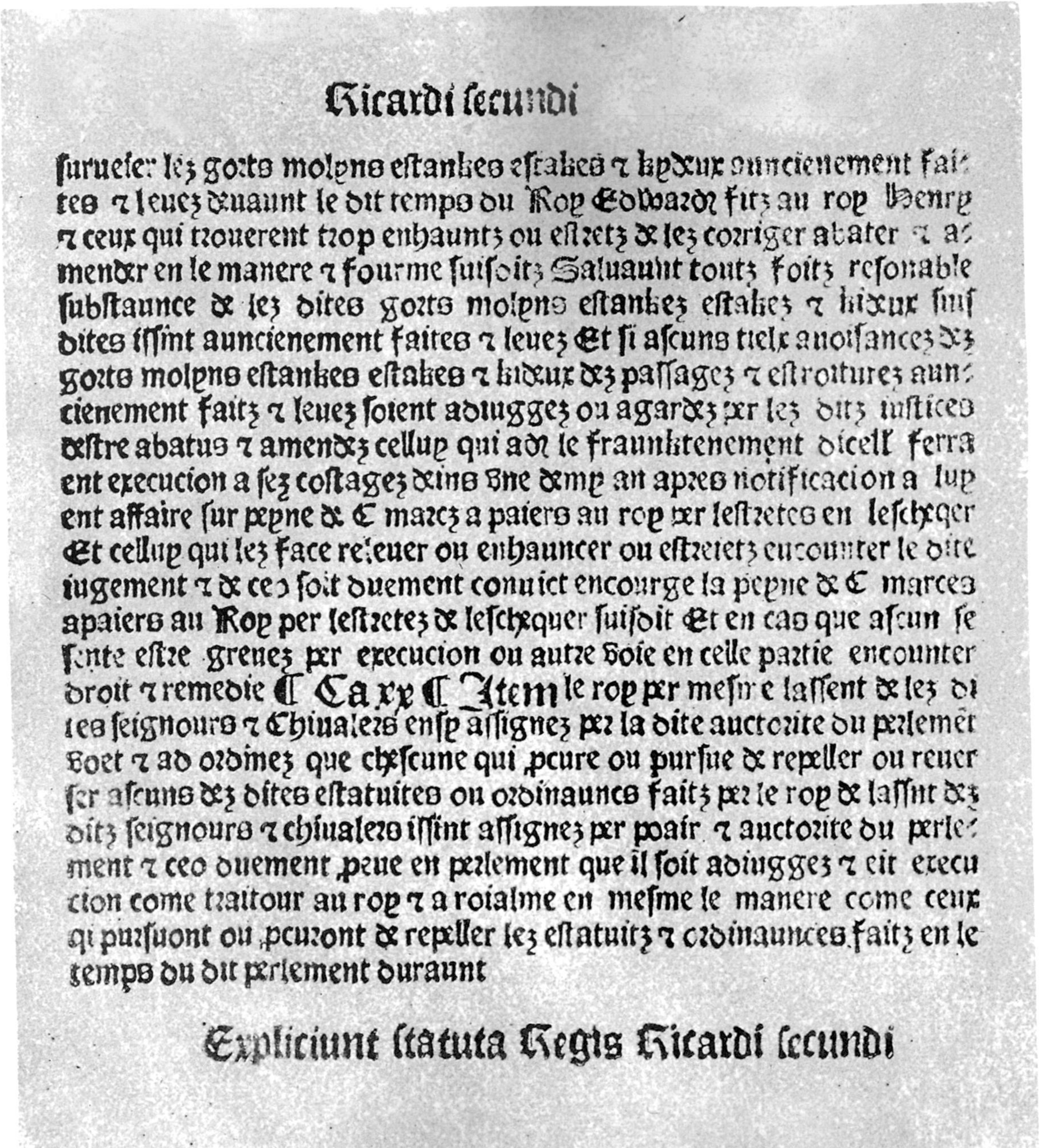

Ricardi secundi

surueier les gortes molyns estankes estakes ⁊ kydeux auncienement faites ⁊ leuez deuaunt le dit temps du Roy Edward fitz au roy Henry
⁊ ceux qui trouerent trop enhauntz ou estretz de les corriger abater ⁊ a-
mender en le manere ⁊ fourme suisoitz Saluaunt toutz foitz resonable
substaunce de les dites gortes molyns estankez estakes ⁊ kidux suis
dites issint auncienement faites ⁊ leuez Et si ascuns tielx anoisances des
gortes molyns estankes estakes ⁊ kideux des passages ⁊ estroiturez auncienement faitz ⁊ leuez soient adiuggez ou agardez per les ditz iustices
destre abatus ⁊ amendez celluy qui ad le fraunktenement dicell ferra
ent execucion a sez costagez deins vne demy an apres notificacion a luy
ent affaire sur peyne de C marcz a paiers au roy per lestretes en lescheqer
Et celluy qui les face reieuer ou enhauncer ou estreietz encounter le dite
iugement ⁊ de ceo soit duement conuict encourge la peyne de C marces
apaiers au Roy per lestretez de lescheqer suisdit Et en cas que ascun se
sente estre greuez per execucion ou autre voie en celle partie encounter
droit ⁊ remedie ¶ Ca xv ¶ Item le roy per mesme lassent des les di
tes seignours ⁊ Chiualers ensy assignez per la dite auctorite du perlement
voet ⁊ ad ordinez que chescune qui pcure ou pursue de repeller ou reuer
ser ascuns des dites estatuites ou ordinaunces faitz per le roy ⁊ lassnt des
ditz seignours ⁊ chiualers issint assignez per poair ⁊ auctorite du perlement ⁊ ceo duement preue en perlement que il soit adiuggez ⁊ eit execu
cion come traitour au roy ⁊ a roialme en mesme le manere come ceux
qi pursuont ou pcuront de repeller les estatuitz ⁊ ordinaunces faitz en le
temps du dit perlement duraunt

Expliciunt statuta Regis Ricardi secundi

FIGURE 8. William Henry Fox Talbot. *Fac-simile of an Old Printed Page*, November 12, 1839. Salted paper print from a photogenic drawing negative; image: 18.6 x 16.7 cm., paper: 22.9 x 18.6 cm.

unaffected, and thus a negative image of the object was formed. In this, Talbot had advanced no further than his predecessors, for the light-sensitive salts remained in the paper.[6] If the image thus formed was viewed under ordinary light, it soon began to darken all over.

Talbot continued his experiments throughout 1834, first at Lacock, and then in the autumn in Geneva. He finally noticed an anomaly: the edges of his coated papers sometimes displayed a different sensitivity than did the centers. Contemplating this, he realized that the ratio of salt to silver affected the sensitivity. Contrary to what might have been expected, a weak solution of salt produced the greatest effect, and a strong solution almost none at all. Talbot then sensitized his paper with a weak solution of salt, made his exposure, and flooded the paper with a strong salt solution. This process converted the remaining light-sensitive silver to a state where it was relatively inert, allowing his pictures to be viewed under normal light. Photography on paper had become a reality.

Talbot privately named this initial process *sciagraphy*—the depiction of objects through their shadows. His first attempts at using this paper in a camera were failures. This initial process would now be classed as a print-out paper, where all of the energy for the reduction of the silver had to come directly from the sunlight. An enormous exposure (as was possible by placing the paper under an object in the sun) made the image visible after some minutes. By the summer of 1835, he had refined this process, attaining a nicety of proportions that allowed him to use it in very small cameras—"mousetraps," as his wife once called them. Exposure times were still very long—about an hour—but the potential had been realized (figure 7).

This process remained private to Talbot and to close family members. He was extraordinarily active in other areas of study during this period. By the time photography was announced to the public in 1839, Talbot had published four books and twenty-seven scientific papers, and had received the Royal Medal from the Royal Society for his work in mathematics. How he rued the day in January 1839 when he learned that a Parisian artist, Louis Jacques Mandé Daguerre, had been the first to publicly announce a photographic process! Talbot hastily displayed his leftover examples from 1835, now calling them photogenic drawings, but Daguerre had taken the day. In the end, it would turn out that their methods were wholly different. The Daguerreotype resulted in a beautiful and highly detailed, unique image on a silver-plated sheet of copper. Talbot's process could produce only shadows on a coarse sheet of paper. He had long realized that this "negative" (a term soon to be applied by Sir John Herschel) could be printed on another sheet of sensitive paper, reversing the tones once again back to their original values. However, he initially viewed this extra step as a disadvantage. It was a tricky procedure, and one that confused the fine details even further.[7]

Throughout 1839 Talbot continued to struggle with his photogenic drawings. While the process remained best suited to contact printing, he began to recognize the value of the negative in enabling multiple prints.[8] The ability to make an exacting *Fac-simile of an Old Printed Page* (figure 8) so excited Talbot that he later included a copy of it as plate IX in his *Pencil of Nature*. Selecting a 1484 black letter treatise on taxes from his own library, Talbot cleverly picked from this volume a sheet printed on the recto only. By shining sunlight through it, he was able to print it by contact onto a sheet of sensitive paper. The resulting negative could then be used to make multiple prints.[9] During the summer of 1840, Talbot's visual sensibilities began to improve under the tutelage of the art he had invented, as the ability to see almost immediately on paper the camera's interpretation of the scene in front of it finally taught him how to observe. During the summer of 1840, by carefully honing his practice of the photogenic drawing process, Talbot was to produce some of his finest negatives.[10] The main drawback was that the exposure times remained long—a minute or two in favorable sunlight was the best that could be hoped for. In interiors, on cloudy days, or in areas deep in shade, the possibilities for adequate exposures were distinctly limited.

In October 1840, during photography's second public year, Talbot made a breakthrough that was almost magical in its character. Within a series of experiments, he found that a solution of gallic acid and silver nitrate would strengthen underexposed negatives to the point where they could be seen. A very brief exposure to light, sometimes just a second or two, would produce no visible effect on the sensitive paper. However, when the sheet was bathed in the developing solution, the invisible latent image triggered by the light was chemically amplified. Within a few seconds, an image of full density could be achieved. This discovery paved the way for most photographs that have been done ever since. Unlike Talbot's original photogenic drawings, print-out processes in which the image emerged from the camera fully formed, the new process produced an apparently blank sheet of paper during its brief exposure. This was then amplified by the chemical developer to reveal the full tones of the image. Called, appropriately, a developed-out process, this approach made Talbot's paper negatives competitive in speed with the rival Daguerreotype. When he patented and publicly announced the new negative process in the spring of 1841, Talbot named it calotype photogenic drawing—soon shortened to simply calotype (or, as his mother and close friends encouraged, the Talbotype).[11] It was this negative process enabling exposures to be made in the range of seconds rather than minutes or hours that finally rendered Talbot's system practical.

Henry Talbot supported his loyal valet, Nicolaas Henneman, in leaving his direct employ to set up the first commercial photographic printing establishment. Located in the town of Reading, it was opened in 1843 specifically to exploit the possibilities of photo-

FIGURE 9.   William Henry Fox Talbot. *Westminster from the Hungerford Market, London across the Thames*, June 1841. Salted paper print; image: 13.3 x 18.3 cm., paper: 18.6 x 22.7 cm.

graphic publishing within the domain traditionally commanded by engravers and lithographers. The plates for Talbot's grand promotional statement, *The Pencil of Nature*, were printed at the Reading Establishment. Each was an original photographic print, hand-coated and exposed to the sun under a negative. Each fascicle of the *Pencil* had several original silver photographic prints mounted in with text, but the whole idea was so new that Talbot found he had to insert an explanatory "Notice to the Reader," explaining that "the plates of the present work are impressed by the agency of Light alone, without any aid whatever from the artist's pencil. They are the sun-pictures themselves, and not, as some persons have imagined, engravings in imitation." The fascicles were sold freely through booksellers, but were produced in steadily diminishing numbers as production difficulties overtook Henneman.[12] Around the time of the first fascicle of *The Pencil of Nature*, Henneman also took on the production of a photographic frontispiece for the privately

Figure 10.   Amelia Elizabeth Guppy. *Utrecht Seals*, 1853? from Phillipps album no. 20976, leaf 14. Salted paper print; image: 20.7 x 16.1 cm., volume: 25.2 x 20.2 cm.

published *Record of the Death-Bed of C.M.W.*[13] During the autumn of 1844, Talbot photographed for a new publication, this one to be sold by subscription, following Sir Walter Scott and titled *Sun Pictures in Scotland*.[14] The prints for all of these were made at Henneman's establishment in Reading. At the end of 1846, Henneman abandoned that location and moved to the larger potential market of London. He carried on the tradition of producing photographic prints for book illustration, making by hand more than 1,650 original prints for William Stirling's 1848 *Annals of the Artists of Spain*, the first book of art history to be illustrated by photography.[15] All of these rare and marvelous publications are represented in the Horblit collection.

With all this activity in publishing, it was almost inevitable that Talbot would sooner or later come to the attention of Sir Thomas Phillipps. Just when and how the two men initially came into contact is not known. Munby claims that they first met in London on May 3, 1843, and that may well have been the first time they came face to face, but an item in the Horblit collection implies a much earlier contact.[16] Arguably the most engaging Talbot image in the collection is a view of London, looking over the busy traffic on the River Thames (figure 9). Dated June 1841 in Talbot's hand, it belongs to a series of views that Talbot took over a two-day period and that is thought to be the earliest surviving paper photographs of London.[17] The view shows Westminster Abbey on the right and a gap before Westminster Hall on the left; the expected Westminster Palace is missing between these, having burnt in 1834 and not having yet been rebuilt at the time of the photograph. Talbot had taken up temporary residence in lodgings in Cecil Street, just behind Kings College (where his friend and colleague Sir Charles Wheatstone had his laboratory) and convenient to the Royal Society's rooms in Somerset House. His mother, Lady Elisabeth Feilding, recorded on June 15, 1841, that she had gone "to see Henry make Calotypes in his new domicile in Cecil Street."[18] Talbot wrote to his wife, Constance, that same day that "my windows in Cecil St. command a good view of the river but unfortunately I find that the London atmosphere prevents a good result, even when the fog is hardly visible to the eye."[19] This difficulty, caused by the excessive sensitivity of Talbot's negative paper to blue light, is evident in the final image. Although no correspondence about this print has been traced, it is entirely possible that Talbot sent Phillipps this image almost immediately: an envelope survives—frustratingly empty—of just the right size, addressed in Talbot's hand to "Sir T. Phillips [sic] Bart. with Mr. Talbot's Compts." Phillipps added the note, "autograph of . . . Talbot Esq discoverer of ~~the~~ Photography ~~drawing~~ — July 1841."[20] It seems quite likely that the London image was conveyed in this envelope. Obviously, neither man knew the other well at this point, but there was every reason for them to become better acquainted in the future.

Given their mutual interests in reproduction and in ancient languages, it is not surprising that Talbot and Phillipps should have maintained a correspondence. On July 30, 1846, Phillipps wrote to Talbot,

> Some time since you were so good as to give me a fac-simile of a deed produced by your Photograph which was so exact that I could have almost believed it to be a *real* Deed—I have often reflected on the important uses to which this may be turned & among others of the preservation of remarkable writing. I have a MS of the 7th Century written in so remarkable a character that it would be well worth the trouble to make a fac-simile of it by means of your discovery & I should be extremely glad if you would come here & look at it & give me your opinion of it—I have lately bought many of your published Views &c by your Pencil of Nature & I begin to think it is almost useless to be at the expense of Line Engraving, when the Picture is given so exactly in two Minutes exhibition to the light.[21]

Talbot replied on August 16, 1846,

> I regret that I am unable to avail myself at present of your kind invitation to Middle Hill to inspect your MSS; but I shall have great pleasure in doing so at another time. Would you like me to send one of my assistants to Middle Hill to copy the MS of the 7th century for you, if it be found copyable, and at the same time he could make views of your house and the surrounding scenery or of any other interesting objects.[22]

Talbot was then staying at nearby Cheltenham, and on August 29, 1846, Phillipps replied,

> I shall be extremely glad if you would send over one of your assistants & as the weather I think is now likely to clear up we shall have more Sun. . . . I should be glad to buy one of your Apparatus, if any are to be sold, & if so, the Assistant could bring it with him.[23]

The assistant Talbot referred to was, in fact, his former valet, Nicolaas Henneman.[24]

Some of the most intriguing and challenging photographs in the Phillipps/Horblit collection were produced by one of the most intriguing people to be inspired by Talbot's invention. They are absolutely perfect reminders of how little we know about the early history of photography and how dependent we are on what at first glance might appear to be some of the less glamorous of the artifacts that might have been preserved. Two albums in the collection are titled *Mrs. Guppy's Photographs at Middle Hill*.[25] In these albums, Sir Thomas treated both paper calotype negatives and salted paper prints as he might have done miscellaneous manuscript leaves, having them sewn in by an edge, naked and unmounted. They are mostly what photographers of the time would have termed wholeplate size (that is, around two-thirds the size of a standard sheet of typing paper). All

FIGURE 11.   Amelia Elizabeth Guppy. *Map of China, Held in a Frame*, 1853? from Phillipps album no. 19044, leaf 8. Calotype negative; image: 22.8 x 18.4 cm., volume: 25 x 20 cm.

taken in a camera, the subjects encompass various ingenious ways by which diverse cultures attempted to record their day-to-day life and to communicate this to posterity (see figures 10, 11, and 12). On looking at the copies of seals, maps, and inscribed urns, one is forcefully struck by how difficult it would have been to bring these to the printed page without the use of photography. Mrs. Guppy was providing Sir Thomas with a means of preserving his collection. This is underscored by some of the most poignant views in the volumes. Showing a disintegrating manuscript, these cautionary images are simply titled *Dust*.

In many ways, Amelia Elizabeth Guppy (1808–1886) was typical of the sort of person whose imagination was captured by photography in its earliest days, but that was perhaps the only way in which she was typical.[26] Born Amelia Parkinson, little is known of her childhood, except that she was raised in an atmosphere of comfortable privilege at Kinnersley Castle in Herefordshire.[27] Amelia was neatly summed up by a granddaughter as a "noted beauty and a toast," a description easily believable from the surviving portraits of her. A more complex picture is available in a description of her granddaughter Ruth, who is said to have closely resembled Amelia:

> Slender and long-legged, quick with life and intelligence, she had a mercurial temperament, at one moment charged with a brittle gaiety, and the next capricious, petulant or withdrawn; but in all moods and at all moments lovely to behold.[28]

The most direct assessment was from the granddaughter who said Amelia "was a lady of wildly independent mould and adventurous spirit, as well as of considerable talent as an artist."[29]

At least some of the artistic influences on this young woman of "considerable talent" are clearly implied. Her mother, Lucy Lechmere Parkinson, was an accomplished artist who erected a kiln on their property in order to fire the windows she painted for the nearby Church of Saint James. Amelia was a pupil of the famous painter and instruction-book writer David Cox. Family tradition has it that he stayed at Kinnersley Castle when he first moved to Herefordshire in 1814. Whether this direct connection is true or not, Cox was soon teaching at Miss Croucher's Girls School in nearby Hereford. Several David Cox paintings remained in the family until well into this century, said to be ones given to his young pupil. Extremely talented in her youth, Amelia may even have been the Miss Parkinson admitted in the unusual capacity of "Honorary Exhibitor" in the Royal Academy exhibitions from 1815 to 1828.[30]

Three threads that would soon be tied together emerged in the year 1834: Henry Talbot achieved his first successes in sciagraphy, slavery was abolished in the British

Empire, and Amelia eloped and got married. It is this latter event that possibly provides a clue to her connection with Sir Thomas Phillipps. Although her family approved of her attachment to Robert Guppy, a promising and energetic lawyer, for some reason the two decided to elope. Their immediate destination was Bitterly Court, the Shropshire home of her cousins the Walcots. Just a decade later, in 1844, the Reverend John Walcot would marry Maria Sophia, Sir Thomas's second daughter.

By all outward appearances, Robert Guppy was the most conservative member of his family, with the rest of the Guppys' seemingly more closely attuned to Amelia's inventive and mercurial temperament. Her husband's parents had made their fortune by inventing the special nail used to attach copper sheathing to the bottoms of British warships. This seemingly trivial invention, which kept the British ships free of barnacles, was a secret weapon decisive in the Napoleonic Wars. It enabled the British ships to sail faster and to stay at sea longer than the French ones, and this contribution made the Guppy family quite wealthy. Although Samuel Guppy held the patent for the nails, it is likely that his wife, Sarah Maria Beach, was at least the co-inventor. She took out other patents, in her own name, for such devices as a special mechanical bed, an attachment that allowed one to cook an egg in the top of a tea urn, and a method for constructing chain suspension bridges.

One of Amelia's new brothers-in-law was Thomas Richard Guppy, an engineer and partner with Isambard Kingdom Brunel. Brunel was to apply Sarah Guppy's method of bridge making to the spectacular Hungerford Bridge in London. Four years after Talbot took his view of *Westminster from the Hungerford Market, London across the Thames* (figure 9), he would return to the same area to record the newly built Hungerford Bridge in one of his most striking images.[31] Guppy was a founder of the Great Western Railway and a builder of Atlantic steamships, including the Great Western. His foundry in Naples fabricated the delightful market in Florence that is still in use today.

Another of Amelia's new brothers-in-law, Samuel, had perhaps the greatest influence on her. A sugar manufacturer, he married Georgina Protheroe, the daughter of a plantation owner in Trinidad. Colonel Philip Protheroe hired Amelia's husband to handle matters arising from the abolition of slavery, and on his visits there, Robert Guppy fell in love with Trinidad. His description to Amelia of two estates of

> luxuriant fertility, of the hills that enfolded them . . . of the rare orchids that grew there . . . made such an instant appeal to his wife's impulsive enthusiasm and love of beauty and adventure that they lost no time in . . . making known their resolve to settle in Trinidad.[32]

F I G U R E 12.　Amelia Elizabeth Guppy. *Babylonian Urn and Fragment of a Stone Figure on Pile of Books from Sir Thomas Phillipps' Library*, 1853, from Phillipps album no. 20976, leaf 25. Calotype negative; image: 21.8 x 17.6 cm., volume: 25.2 x 20.2 cm.

In 1839, the year in which the invention of photography was announced to the public, Robert gave up his promising London practice, Amelia placed their three small children in the care of relatives in England, and they moved away from the society in which Amelia had flourished. At first, their new life was idyllic. Amelia

> bought a white mule and a chestnut pony: the former for herself to ride, the latter for Thorpe, then a young man, whom she engaged as her personal attendant, and followed by whom, weighted down with her artistic paraphernalia, she explored the surrounding countryside. Where she elected to sketch he would set up her easel, and stand behind the stool on which she sat, holding a vast green-lined parasol over her head.[33]

In time,

> for miles around San Fernando she became a familiar figure, mounted on her white mule, clad in her riding-habit with its tight-fitting jacket and long flowing skirt, a wide-brimmed hat upon her head, a floating veil about her face, a jabot of lace at her throat and yellow gauntlets upon her hands; attended always by the faithful Thorpe astride the pony, carrying the painting equipment and the green-lined parasol. There was something remote and exotic in her appearance, yet everything also of the *grande dame*.[34]

Soon this all began to sour. Robert Guppy was an idealist who had personally invested in the future of a Trinidad without slavery and he defended that position throughout his legal career. What he could not defend against, however, was the enormous economic disruption brought about by the change from a slave to a laborer economy. Profits vanished, and once-grand plans had to be scaled back. Amelia might well have adapted to this parsimony if other things had remained equal, but they did not.

> At San Fernando . . . apart from her painting, there was little to capture her mind or imagination. She missed the intellectual and artistic stimulus of the circles in which she had moved in England, and found her society restricted to that of people whose interests and outlook were severely limited. Their narrow preoccupations were as wearisome to her as the scope of her intelligence was intimidating to them. She found them boring and tedious, and they found her incomprehensible and alarming.[35]

It was at some point during this period of only partial accommodation to life in Trinidad that Amelia took up the new art of photography. It had been introduced to the public in 1839, the same year she had moved to the island, but where and exactly when she acquired her interest in photography is not known. The earliest known photograph ascribed to her is a calotype portrait of her son, Robert Lechmere Guppy (within a few years, Lechmere, as he was universally known, was to be the first to describe Trinidad's "millions fish." The popular aquarium fish is named in his honor). The portrait was done in 1847, while Lechmere was still being raised in England, so it must have been during a visit by Amelia to her original home. The choice of a portrait as subject was perhaps more significant than simply being a family snapshot. Theodora Walter remembered that "Grandma Guppy . . . was quite a well known artist in her day, especially as a portrait painter," so the genre would have been familiar to her, even if the medium was new. No other portraits by her have been located.

There was nothing to keep an independent spirit like Amelia from being self-taught in photography, but it would have been not uncommon for someone like her to receive some initial help from an adept already familiar with the vagaries of the art. Family lore records that Amelia was a personal friend of Talbot's. This may be true, but the extensive archives of Lacock Abbey (not yet fully processed) have yielded no mention of her thus far.[36] Until at least the late eighteenth century, there were Guppys in Melksham, the village adjacent to Lacock, and it is possible that Amelia's in-laws maintained ties there, however distant that branch of the family had become.[37] Another possible connection is a slight hint in the visitors' book kept by Talbot's mother, Lady Elisabeth Feilding. She recorded the 1829 visit of a Mr. Protheroe, perhaps someone from the family of Amelia's brother-in-law Samuel.[38] It may even have been Samuel himself who taught Amelia photography. Although none of his own photographs has been traced with certainty,[39] when he died in 1876, the editor of the *British Journal of Photography* honored him as "one of the oldest of amateurs."[40] Samuel's life was as colorful as that of any of the Guppys. His 1863 book, *Mary Jane; or Spiritualism Chemically Explained*, is filled with scenes of wonder. It is based on experiences with his first wife, Georgina Protheroe, whose "control" was named Mary Jane.[41] The book's direct references to photography are various. Although Guppy's linking of the efforts of Jacob in the Book of Genesis with the accomplishments of Louis Jacques Mandé Daguerre might seem obscure to the modern mind, the author clearly had both practical experience in photography and a greater than usual knowledge of its early history.[42] Georgina died shortly after this, and Samuel's reputation was assured by his second marriage, to the famous medium Agnes Nichol. She was the only major spiritualist of her day never detected to be a fraud. Samuel Guppy must have come into contact with another English spiritualist, Henry Collen, a miniature painter and friend of Talbot's who took out the very first license to practice photographic portraiture in London.[43] It might even have been Collen who taught Amelia Guppy. Another possible connection to the art is indicated by her son Lechmere Guppy, the subject of her earliest known photograph. He was later to publish with Jabez Hogg, an eye surgeon who was also an early advocate of photography (and a bitter opponent of Talbot's patents).[44] Finally, there is a remote possibility that Amelia Guppy came under the same artistic influences as Lady Clementina Hawarden, a noted early photographic artist.[45]

Amelia Guppy is acknowledged only twice in the published records of the organized photographic circles. The 1859 list of members of London's Photographic Society includes "Guppy. Mrs. Amelia Elizabeth. *San Fernando, Trinidad*."[46] The only exhibition records traced of her work are from 1854, when she submitted four landscape calotypes to the first annual exhibition of the Photographic Society in London. Her chosen subjects were *Stoke Bay Castle*, a *Garden House*, *Druid's Oak*, and *Ludlow Castle Entrance*.[47] Many of her paper negatives survived into this century, but only one has been found recently in the family collections. However, these collections retain numerous salt prints made from calotype negatives, the subjects of which are similar to those that she exhibited in 1854. Although undated, they are entirely consistent with photography of this period. One previously unidentified salt print in the collection of the Royal Photographic Society in Bath matches one of the family-owned prints. Curiously, no photographs made by her in Trinidad are known. It is possible, although counterintuitive, that she restricted this activity to her frequent visits to England.

We do not know why Phillipps chose Amelia Guppy in particular to photograph some items in his collection. Whatever the reason, whether it was simply a matter of opportunity or a carefully planned selection, she was a good choice. Her surviving architectural views demonstrate an excellent mastery of detail and an intelligent use of natural light (for all practical purposes, all that was available to photography at the time). The large and irregular Map of China (figure 11), executed on silk (?), had to be stretched on a crude frame and taken outdoors in order to be properly lit. Once there, it could be treated by her in the same manner as an ancient doorway or a section of a wall. But, rather than being forced to wait for the sun to achieve the best position, the map could have been rotated until the light favored its reproduction. What was required was a uniform light, emphasizing content of what was on the map's surface rather than its texture. The exposure time in the camera was perhaps a minute or two if the light was cooperating. While fine for a portrait of a stone building, a time this long would have demanded that careful attention be paid to the wind, lest the delicately stretched map flutter during the exposure, ruining the precise detail so necessary to the task at hand.

The collections of Utrecht Seals (figure 10) posed a different set of photographic challenges. These were small enough to have been photographed indoors on a library table and the extended exposure time needed would have posed little problem. The light had to be severely raking in order to create the shadows that would define the intaglio impressions. However, these very shadows would have confounded the effect if not carefully controlled. The tray of seals was probably rotated to achieve the most favorable angle of light, and it is likely that Amelia Guppy also reflected some additional light back onto them to bring them within range. Talbot had counseled doing this in the text to plate five of his *Pencil of Nature*. Describing a copy of his plaster *Bust of Patroclus*, Talbot wrote,

> These delineations are susceptible of an almost unlimited variety, . . . the directness or obliquity of the illumination causing of course an immense difference in the effect . . . a better effect is obtained by delineating them in cloudy weather than in sunshine. For, the sunshine causes such strong shadows as sometimes to confuse the subject. To prevent this, it is a good plan to hold a white cloth on one side of the statue at a little distance to reflect back the sun's rays and cause a faint illumination of the parts which would otherwise be lost in shadow.

From both pictorial and cultural points of view, the most extraordinary images in these two volumes are the series depicting Babylonian urns and modern books (figure 12). The setting is transparently clear. A simple wooden chair has been brought out into the garden and positioned to catch the best angle of light. A heavily inscribed Babylonian urn displays its incisions in three-dimensional relief. A fragment of a sculpted hand raised above other incised writing brings in another culture's form of writing. The striped cushion of the chair poses two problems: it is visually distracting and would have formed a poor support for the heavy and irregularly shaped objects. Both of these objections are overcome by the simple strategy of placing the objects on top of two large leather-bound books brought out from the library, isolating the stripes and giving a level foundation. Or is it all that neat and simple? I don't think so. The juxtaposition of the ancient forms of recording —marks made in wet clay or stone—with printed books is in itself suggestive. It is all the more evocative when one considers that both of these stages are being contrasted with the very medium that is recording them. Mrs. Guppy's photograph absorbs these earlier cultural expressions, captures them, transforms them, and thus extends their life through its own magic.

All in all, the images Mrs. Guppy executed for Sir Thomas Phillipps are extraordinary documents of photography, demonstrating its virtues in precise reproduction. We do not know how long she continued working in the medium of photography. In 1871, at the age of sixty-three, Amelia Guppy set off on her own to explore the upper reaches of Venezuela's Orinoco River, with the goal of painting and collecting orchids. By one account, "its rapids were phenomenally dangerous, its jungles dense, forbidding and fever ridden, and its native Indians were notoriously savage and unpredictable in their behaviour."[48] No exaggeration, surely, for the source of this river remained undiscovered until

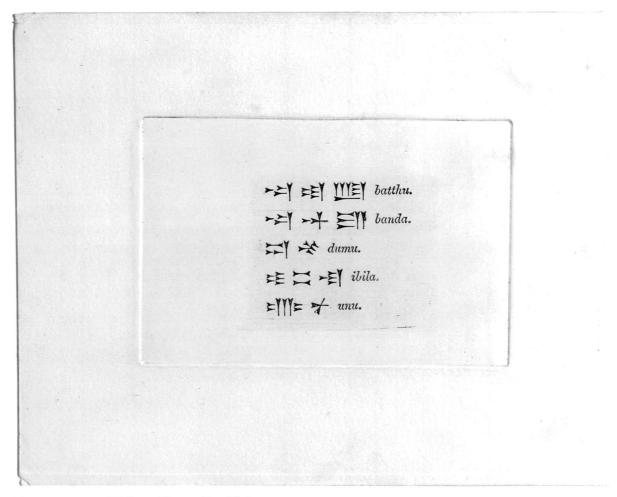

FIGURE 13.   William Henry Fox Talbot. *Assyrian Cuneiform Writing with Translations*, 1874?
Photoglyphic engraving; plate: 6.5 x 9.7 cm., paper: 12.6 x 16.1 cm.

1951, eight decades after Amelia's solitary journey. She was gone for more than a year, so alarming her family that her son Francis went looking for her. Tragically, he died of fever on the trip without ever finding his mother, who returned safely on her own. The collection of orchids that she brought back lasted into the twentieth century. The marvelous series of watercolors she created on this pioneering journey, mostly of flowers, survived until 1945. They were burnt by a descendant who felt their paper had deteriorated through insect attack beyond value, much to the chagrin of other family members. More of her work was lost when it was put in storage on Trinidad during the Second World War (not through enemy action; the family's effects simply disappeared from the warehouse).

Amelia Elizabeth Guppy died on July 27, 1886, at Belmont, Port of Spain, Trinidad. Sadly, she died alone, for her family was all visiting England at the time. She died as she had lived, a spirit displaced, poignantly described as an "old woman burned out by her own flame."[49]

In a sense, many of the early paper photographs that Phillipps preserved and Horblit later collected were likewise burnt out by their own flame. Many of them are heavily faded, ghostly reminders of once-glorious tones. The causes of this deterioration are both external and internal. The image is composed of a delicate deposit of fine silver trapped in the surface fibers of the paper, unprotected by any sort of overcoating. The same sulfurous fumes that cause silverware to tarnish also attack the silver photographic image, but whereas the slight layer of tarnish on a fork does no sensible damage to the mass of solid silver, it is relatively more destructive to the microscopically thin silver image. The salted paper prints (more natural for the human eye to translate than the negatives) are actually generally more susceptible to this destructive chemical process than are the negatives. The printed-out silver clusters deposited on the positives are extremely fine in their division and very vulnerable. In contrast, the chemically developed negatives have larger silver clusters, giving some natural protection against the outside world. Moreover, negatives were rarely trimmed and mounted down on board (a practice that necessarily would end their utilitarian if not their visual life). The use of wood-pulp papers and boards was on the rise at the time when photography was introduced. Many of these were highly acidic. When the paste from a dubious pot was slathered on the back of a print to be mounted, it brought its own chemical soup to the table, as well as furnishing a convenient solvent (water) that could leech additional chemicals from the mounting board. On the whole, therefore, prints and negatives kept loose in portfolios enjoyed a better and longer life.

But it was the internal environment of these early photographs that was often the more damaging factor. Talbot's initial approaches to making his photographs permanent were what would now be termed stabilization processes. They neutralized much of the light-sensitivity of the silver salts but did not remove the salts themselves. Each of these photographs that survives, in whatever state of readability, is a miracle of historic preservation.[50] The hypo fixer that Talbot adopted from his friend Sir John Herschel's practice was a great improvement in that it removed the remaining light-sensitive salts entirely from the paper. Most of the surviving photographs from Talbot's era certainly most of those produced from 1840 onward were fixed in hypo. Yet this elixir was a finicky and demanding mistress. Properly compounded, properly applied, and fully washed out in copious amounts of water, it did its work well. However, chemical purity was hardly a given in

Talbot's day. Adequate supplies of clean water were often difficult to come by, and then expensive fuel had to be burnt to heat the water to the temperature required for it to be effective in its solvent action.[51]

By the time of the Great Exhibition in 1851, Henry Talbot had come to recognize that his art was cursed by original sin. Rather than being discouraged by this, however, he conceived a new way to get nature to make his drawings for him. Building on a series of experiments dating back to 1838, Talbot took out a patent in 1852 for a process that he called photographic engraving. This is the direct predecessor of the photogravure process used to this day. When a sensitized layer of gelatin was spread on a conventional steel plate, exposure to light under a photographic positive created a physical mask in the pattern of the original image. When etched by conventional means, an intaglio plate could be printed in a conventional press, using good paper and time-tested carbon-based inks. In 1858, Talbot patented another, greatly improved process for making the printing plates and called it photoglyphic engraving. This new approach incorporated a resin aquatint ground that did a much better job of retaining middle tones. Perhaps more important, Talbot devised the system of using various concentrations of ferric chloride as etchants, an innovation universally adopted in the printing industry, not only for photogravure but for all forms of gravure printing. It is employed to this day, largely by practitioners who have no idea that the inventor of this critical working tool was also the inventor of photography. Around 1866, Talbot incorporated further refinements in a process he called photosculpsit.[52] Only his death, in 1877, put an end to Talbot's enormous contributions to this promising new technology. He had finally merged his world of the sun with the domain of the printing press. Sir Thomas Phillipps recognized the value of these efforts and began collecting Talbot's photogravures. The copy of a printed translation of Assyrian Cuneiform (figure 13) furnishes yet another example of one medium being used to extend another.[53]

On April 29, 1861, Phillipps wrote to Talbot, thanking him

> for the really, (without flattery,) beautiful specimen of Photographic Engraving which you have sent to me. The lines are so distinct & clear without blotting, that it looks as if laid on by Electrotype. If your process is perfected without being very costly it will supersede all other modes of multiplying copies . . . for it appears to me that the strokes in your Engraving are much finer than anastatic printing could make them.[54]

Sir Thomas was not far off the mark. Shortly after his lifetime, Talbot was proven correct in the direction of his quest, when other photogravure processes based on his emerged as powerful companions of type. Within the twentieth century, even the printed word yielded to the lure of photography, as cold type replaced the traditional hot lead, and both pictures and words came to be reproduced using Talbot's invention. The famous bibliophile would have liked that, as would the inventor himself.

In preserving and building on the fine collection of photography started by Sir Thomas Phillipps, Harrison Horblit ensured that the legacy of the young medium would be preserved for future study, in much the same style as was done by Phillipps himself for the manuscript. Sometimes pale on the surface in their old age, these "splendid calotypes" possess an unequivocal inner beauty. They are eloquent testimony to the earliest harnessing of the sun to make images. In reviewing the first number of Talbot's *Pencil of Nature*, the *Athenaeum* astutely observed that photography had "enabled us to hand down to future ages a picture of the sunshine of yesterday."[55] Sir Thomas Phillipps and Harrison Horblit both did their part to keep that light alive.

NOTES

1. Pauline Trevelyan's diary entry for April 9, 1845. MS C133 v. 25. Kenneth Spencer Research Library, University of Kansas at Lawrence.

2. Talbot, letter to Sir John Herschel, March 21, 1839. Herschel Collection, The Royal Society, London.

3. Larry J. Schaaf, *H. Fox Talbot's The Pencil of Nature: Anniversary Facsimile* (New York: Hans P. Kraus, Jr., Inc., 1989).

4. There are two excellent biographies of Talbot, different in their emphasis but complementary in their character. The standard work is H. J. P. Arnold, *William Henry Fox Talbot: Pioneer of Photography and Man of Science* (London: Hutchinson Benham, 1977). The other, which places more emphasis on Talbot's visual productions, is Gail Buckland, *Fox Talbot and the Invention of Photography* (Boston: David R. Godine, 1980).

5. See Larry J. Schaaf, *Tracings of Light: Sir John Herschel & the Camera Lucida* (San Francisco: The Friends of Photography, 1989). For more on artistic attainments within Talbot's family, see Martin Kemp, "Talbot and the Picturesque View: Henry, Caroline and Constance," *History of Photography* 21, no. 4 (Winter 1997): 270–82.

6. There is a long history of attempts by various people to accomplish much the same thing. Most of these were never made public in a timely fashion, but some undoubtedly took place. See Larry J. Schaaf, "The First Fifty Years of British Photography: 1794–1844," in Michael Pritchard, ed., *Technology and Art: The Birth and Early Years of Photography* (Bath: The Royal Photographic Society, 1990), 9–18.

7. The struggles Talbot went through to win public recognition of his accomplishments are detailed in Larry J. Schaaf, *Out of the Shadows: Herschel, Talbot & the Invention of Photography* (New Haven and London: Yale University Press, 1992).

8. A brief summary of the stages of Talbot's experimentation can be found in Larry J. Schaaf, "'A Wonderful Illustration of Modern Necromancy': Significant Talbot Experimental Prints in the J. Paul Getty Museum," in *Photography, Discovery and Invention* (Malibu: The J. Paul Getty Museum, 1990), 31–46.

9. A portfolio once owned by Phillipps (no. 21009) and now in the Horblit collection contains a number of paper negatives made by contact from a manuscript. Because the original was written on both sides, a reversed shadow of the writing on the verso was recorded when the sunlight was transmitted through the sheet. In a brave but futile attempt to compensate for this effect, the anonymous photographer who produced these (was it Phillipps himself?) struggled to retouch in ink all the spurious information.

10. For examples of this brief but fruitful period, see Larry J. Schaaf, *Sun Pictures Catalogue Seven: Photogenic Drawings by William Henry Fox Talbot* (New York: Hans P. Kraus, Jr., Inc., 1995).

11. Talbot's research thinking can be examined in the facsimile of his notebooks by Larry J. Schaaf, *Records of the Dawn of Photography: Talbot's Notebooks P & Q* (Cambridge: Cambridge University Press, 1996).

12. A surprising number of the originals survive. See Larry J. Schaaf, "Henry Fox Talbot's *The Pencil of Nature*: A Revised Census of Original Copies," *History of Photography* 17, no. 4 (Winter 1993): 388–96.

13. This thirty-three-page, privately published volume, dedicated to Catherine Mary Walter (1819–1844), was written by her brother, John Walter, Jr., who was later to become editor of the *Times*. The text was printed in London by Gilbert & Rivington, undoubtedly in very small numbers. Walter dated his personal statement January 24, 1844, and this date has led to some confusion. The idea has taken hold that this privately printed work predated *The Pencil of Nature*. Although Talbot certainly would not have minded if it had—the real purpose for producing *The Pencil of Nature* was precisely to encourage such publications—it is highly unlikely that the smaller volume was truly so early. Vernon Snow, in "The First Photographically Illustrated Book," *Times Literary Supplement*, December 23, 1965, took this date to be the date of publication. This assumption was repeated in Arthur Gill's otherwise excellent "Record of C.M.W.," *The Photographic Journal*, (October 1975): 490–91. No records of this publication have been traced. The Walters' home of Bear Wood was near Nicolaas Henneman's

establishment in Reading, and it is likely that arrangements for this special production were made in person. On May 31, 1844, just three weeks before the first fascicle of *The Pencil of Nature* was actually issued, Henneman wrote to Talbot, that "I went to Mr. Walter the other day but owing to the weather I did not get such good results as I expected w^yl there I took another Negative of the Bust and Mr. Walter is very much pleased with the result. Mr. Lovejoy advised me not to accept anything if they offer it to mee [sic] thinking it will be more to the advantage for the Calotype" (LA42-32, Fox Talbot Museum, Lacock). If Henneman heeded the advice of the well-known bookseller George Lovejoy, and he probably did, it would explain why no dated invoice has been traced. The prints for *C.M.W.* would not have been made much before this letter, and most likely later than it. By the time they were sent to London and mounted in the printed books, the first fascicle of *The Pencil* would almost certainly have been available to the public. The original bust that Henneman copied was displayed for many years in the lobby of the Times Building, and more recently has been deposited in the Church of Saint Catherine in Bear Wood (built by John Walter in memory of his daughter and consecrated in 1846).

14. The best analysis of this publication is Graham Smith's "William Henry Fox Talbot's Views of Loch Katrine," *Bulletin of the Museums of Art and Archaeology, The University of Michigan* 7 (1984–85): 48–77.

15. The context for this is well covered in Anthony Hamber's pioneering "A Higher Branch of the Art": *Photographing the Fine Arts in England, 1839–1880* (Amsterdam: Gordon and Breach, 1996), 74–76; 143–44.

16. A. N. L. Munby, *The Formation of the Phillipps Library from 1841 to 1872* (Cambridge: Cambridge University Press, 1956), 39.

17. Gavin Stamp analyzes this image in his *The Changing Metropolis: Earliest Photographs of London, 1839–1879* (London: Viking Books, 1984), 28. Stamp illustrates the NMPFT (Science Museum) copy. A second copy is in the Fox Talbot Museum, Lacock, and a third in a private collection. All are terribly faded. *Schaaf no. 3705.*

18. Lady Elisabeth Feilding, *Diary 1841*. Lacock Abbey Collections.

19. Letter, Henry Talbot to Constance Talbot, June 15, 1841. LA41-39, Fox Talbot Museum, Lacock.

20. Gen 1952/3, Special Collections, Edinburgh University Library.

21. Quoted in Munby, *The Formation of the Phillipps Library*, 39–40.

22. Letter, Talbot to Phillipps, August 16, 1846, marked "Answd 19 Aug." C. 496, ff. 163–64, MS Phillipps-Robinson, Bodleian Library, Oxford.

23. Letter, Phillipps to Talbot, August 29, 1846. Fox Talbot Museum, Lacock.

24. In his reply of September 2, Talbot said of his assistant that "he resides at Reading." On December 15, he noted, "My photographer is about to open an establishment on Regent Street." Both of these references clearly describe Nicolaas Henneman. C 496, ff. 165–71, MS Phillipps-Robinson, Bodleian Library, Oxford.

25. The Robinson typescript inventory lists three albums in one lot: "Phillipps MSS. 19044, 20976 and 21009. These three volumes (two of them inscribed by Sir Thomas Phillipps 'Mrs. Guppy's Photographs at Middle Hill' and 'Mrs. Guppy's Photographs of Middle Hill MSS. etc.') comprise a total of about 120 calotype (i.e., Talbotype) photographs *both* positive and negative, and consisting of pictures of manuscripts, charters, seals, specimens of ancient calligraphy, etc. Numbered throughout by Sir Thomas Phillipps and with, in many cases, explanatory titles in his hand. Where the paper is watermarked the date is 1850. An extraordinary collection and possibly THE EARLIEST COLLECTION OF BIBLIOGRAPHICAL PHOTOGRAPHS. This 'Mrs. Guppy' is possibly the assistant of Fox Talbot who Sir Thomas asked Fox Talbot for in a letter of July, 1846 and to whom Fox Talbot referred in a reply dated December the same year (see *Phillipps Studies* IV, pp. 39–40)." It is clear from this description that only two of the albums were marked by Phillipps as being by Mrs. Guppy; these are currently *album no. 12* (Phillipps no. 19044) and *album no. 13* (Phillipps no. 20976). The third album in this grouping, *album no. 11* (Phillipps no. 21009), was clearly not identified in this list as having been associated with Mrs. Guppy. Robinson's speculation about the possible identity of Henry Talbot's assistant is incorrect; see note 24 above.

26. Most of the information on Amelia Guppy is derived from archives held by her descendants. The content of these unpublished sources is largely summarized in Yseult Bridges, edited and completed by Nicholas Guppy, *Child of the Tropics: Victorian Memoirs* (London: Collins and Harvill Press, 1980), a copy of which may be found in the Harvard University Library. This was later reissued in a slightly corrected edition (Port of Spain, Trinidad: Aquarela Galleries, 1988). Unattributed quotations that follow are from the family manuscript sources used for Bridges's volume. I am indebted to Nicholas and Anna Guppy, Geoffrey MacLean, and Constantine Guppy for their assistance and cooperation.

27. She was born on November 21, 1808, at Bullingham Court, Herefordshire, the daughter of Richard Parkinson (d. 1851) and Lucy Lechmere (d. 1834). Her maternal grandparents were the Admiral William Lechmere (1752–1815) and Elizabeth, the daughter of Sir John Dashwood King of West Wycombe. She had one brother, John (1810–1859), who inherited Kinnersley Castle but sold it in 1858.

28. Bridges/Guppy, *Child of the Tropics*, 36.

29. Ibid., 71.

30. Algernon Graves lists various views done by Miss Parkinson, a painter, in most years in this range. Graves, *The Royal Academy of Arts: A Complete Dictionary of Contributors and Their Work from Its Foundation in 1769 to 1904* (London: Henry Graves and Co., Ltd, 1905), 5:58–59.

31. Talbot's view of the Hungerford Suspension Bridge is illustrated in Larry Schaaf, *Sun Pictures Catalogue Three: The Harold White Collection of Works by William Henry Fox Talbot* (New York: Hans P. Kraus, Jr., Inc., 1987), pl. 48. When the bridge was taken down, in the 1860s, the chains were recycled and used to complete the Clifton Suspension Bridge, adjacent to Sarah Guppy's hometown of Bristol, where their splendor can be enjoyed to this day.

32. Bridges/Guppy, *Child of the Tropics*, 73.

33. Ibid.

34. Ibid., 75–76.

35. Ibid., 75.

36. A good indication of the range of potential Talbot sources can be gleaned from Mike Weaver's *Henry Fox Talbot: Selected Texts and Bibliography* (Oxford: Clio Press, 1992). The extent of Talbot's surviving correspondence can be seen in the more than ten thousand letters listed in Larry J. Schaaf's *The Correspondence of William Henry Fox Talbot: A Draft Calendar* (Glasgow: Glasgow University Library Studies, 1995).

37. See Henry Brougham Guppy, *Homes of Family Names in Great Britain* (London: Harrison & Sons, 1890), 397.

38. Elisabeth Feilding, "Visitors at Laycock Abbey," 1827–1846. Lacock Abbey Collections.

39. There is one salt print of Ludlow in the Mowbray-Green Collection in the Bath Reference Library, Bath, England. It was removed from an album in recent times and is labeled in a modern hand as being by a "Mr. Guppy." It seems to be very much in the style of work accomplished by Mrs. Guppy, but no way could be found to confirm the accuracy of the transcription.

40. J. Traill Taylor, *The British Journal Photographic Almanac 1876*, 22. Samuel Guppy was born on November 25, 1795 and died on January 18, 1875. Obituaries also appeared in *The Times* and in the *Spiritual Magazine*.

41. The full title is *Mary Jane; or, Spiritualism Chemically Explained with Spirit Drawings. Also Essays by, and Ideas (Perhaps Erroneous) of, "a Child at School"* (London: printed by John King & Co., 1863). The Harvard University Library has an inscribed copy of this volume.

42. The reference to Genesis 30, verses 37 to 41, appears on page 96. There are frequent other references to photography, including, on page 5, "Photography has opened a new volume in nature;" on page 9, "Suppose a circular room, paper[ed] with photographic sensitive paper," on page 95, "Another important matter is that (as every photographer knows) . . .;" and on page 98, "When Niepce began the study of photography it was based on the discoloration of bitumen by light."

43. Collen was quite active in promoting Talbot's process in the early years. See Larry J. Schaaf, "Henry Collen and the Treaty of Nanking," *History of Photography* 6, no. 4 (October 1982): 353–66; and "Addenda to 'Henry Collen and the Treaty of Nanking,'" *History of Photography* 7, no. 2 (April–June 1983): 163–65.

44. Possibly the son met Hogg through a connection already established by his mother. Robert Lechmere Guppy and Jabez Hogg, "On the Lingual Dentition of Some West Indian Gasteropoda," *Transactions of the Linnean Society*, 1867. For more on Hogg, see Helmut and Alison Gernsheim, *The History of Photography* (New York: McGraw-Hill, 1969), 145, 543.

45. Some years later, Amelia's first cousin Caroline Anna Murray Ogle would marry the Fifth Viscount Hawarden, whose older brother, the Fourth Viscount, was the husband of Lady Clementina Hawarden. Although this was likely just a coincidence, it is possible that the families knew each other prior to that, or moved in similar social circles. For more on Hawarden, see Virginia Dodier, "Clementina, Viscountess Hawarden: Studies from Life," in Mike Weaver, ed., *British Photography in the Nineteenth Century: The Fine Art Tradition* (Cambridge: Cambridge University Press, 1989), 141–50.

46. *List of Members of The Photographic Society* (London: printed by Taylor & Francis, 1859), 9.

47. John Dillwyn Llewelyn (who married Talbot's favorite cousin, Emma) annotated his copy of the printed catalogue and seemed to be familiar with Mrs. Guppy's work. He corrected the entry for 163. *Stoke Bay Castle*, listed as being from a collodion negative, to a Talbotype negative, and inserted the missing information for 204. *Garden House, calotype, Mrs. Guppy*, in *Photographic Society, Exhibition of Photographs and Daguerreotypes* (London: printed by Taylor and Francis, 1854). Llewelyn's annotated copy is now in the collection of the National Museum of Wales, Cardiff.

48. Bridges/Guppy, *Child of the Tropics*, 76.

49. Ibid., 77.

50. An excellent discussion of this is Mike Ware's *Mechanisms of Image Deterioration in Early Photographs: The Sensitivity to Light of W. H. F. Talbot's Halide-Fixed Images, 1834–1844* (London: The Science Museum, 1994).

51. The problems that Nicolaas Henneman faced in producing prints at his Reading Establishment are detailed in Larry J. Schaaf's introductory volume to the facsimile *Pencil of Nature*; especially pp. 38–42.

52. The available literature on this is poor. The best from a technical point of view is Eugene Ostroff's pair of articles, "Etching, Engraving & Photography: History of Photomechanical Reproduction," *The Journal of Photographic Science* 17, no. 1 (1969): 65–80; "Photography and Photogravure: History of Photomechanical Reproduction," *The Journal of Photographic Science* 17, no. 4 (1969): 101–115.

53. Based solely on its appearance and level of technical accomplishment, this photoglyphic engraving would most reasonably be dated to the late 1850s. However, John Huehnergard, Professor of Semitic Philology at Harvard University, has kindly pointed out that four of the signs first appear in Talbot's "Four New Syllabaries and a Bilingual Tablet," *Transactions of the Society of Biblical Archaeology* 3 (1874): 496–529. Talbot's article was based on a fragment of a tablet brought from Nineveh to England in the summer of 1874 by Talbot's friend George Smith. Thus, this photoglyphic engraving must have been made in 1874 or later, near the end of Talbot's life.

54. Letter, Phillipps to Talbot, April 29, 1846. LA61-86, Fox Talbot Museum, Lacock.

55. *Athenaeum*, February 22, 1845, 202.

THE REGARD OF MUNDANE MIRACLES:
THE DAGUERREOTYPE COLLECTION
OF HARRISON D. HORBLIT

Grant B. Romer

Harrison D. Horblit's reputation as a collector of photography derives chiefly from his acquisitions of early paper-based photographs, particularly the work of William Henry Fox Talbot and his circle. Relatively few scholars had the opportunity to visit Horblit and view his collection during his lifetime, but those who did invariably spoke enthusiastically about the richness of his British photographic holdings. Lacking direct access to the collection, many scholars simply assumed that Horblit was an Anglophile and an adherent of that type of historical chauvinism which assigns the invention of photography to one country, one process, and one person. Correspondingly, many concluded that the daguerreotype was excluded from his collecting agenda. A public exhibition of selections from his collection in 1989 did little to dispel this latter supposition since it only included a few examples of the form.

With Mrs. Jean Horblit's gift of the collection and its subsequent transfer to the Houghton Library, knowledge began to spread about its broader contents. Perhaps most surprising of all was the news that it contained 3,141 daguerreotypes, nearly 40 percent of the total photographs in the collection. Horblit had evidently harbored a serious interest in the process; the sheer number of his holdings makes his one of the world's largest daguerreotype collections, and certainly the largest assembled by one collector in this century. In light of Horblit's reputation as a collector of the first rank, expectations of a veritable Aladdin's Cave of daguerreian wonder ran high among daguerreotype enthusiasts. Horblit was a sophisticated man of means, capable of acquiring the rarest, choicest, and most significant daguerreotypes in great number. In the period when he was active, more daguerreotypes than ever before appeared on the market, many of them possessed of precisely those qualities most prized by daguerreotype connoisseurs. Prices, too, were modest compared with those of recent years. It therefore seemed very likely that Horblit had built one of the most sensational daguerreotype collections—if not *the* most sensational—of all time.

Preconceptions of the collection's riches were based upon the type of imagery featured in recent exhibitions, publications, and auctions: portraits of blacks, Indians, Polynesians, and Asians, both real and pretend; souvenirs of gamblers, frontiersmen, gold miners, soldiers, sailors, firemen, doctors, actors, daguerreotypists, dancers, musicians, and clowns, of fat boys, giants, midgets, dwarves, blind men, invalids, and the deceased, of cats, dogs, chickens, horses, mules, oxen, lions, parrots, and elephants, alive and stuffed; pictures of carriages, carts, wagons, canalboats, and sailing and steam-powered ships; nudes; allegorical tableaux; enigmatic still-lifes, sequential narratives; views topographical, pictorial, and journalistic; decorative vignettes, elaborate hand-colored efforts; masterworks of famous studios and celebrity portraiture—in short, all the types of unusual daguerreian sugarplums that dance in the heads of today's collectors, curators, dealers, and auctioneers, the "commodity" images that promise the peculiar type of thrill particular to this medium.

The first few experts to gain privileged access to the collection came to it in a state of great anticipatory excitement, expecting to come face to face with what is described, in the common parlance of daguerreotype dealers, as "stunning," "eye-popping," "mind-blowing," "killer," and "to-die-for" imagery. The anticipation was enhanced, of course, by the knowledge that it would all be "fresh," full of that addicting extra kick that daguerreian discovery provides. Ready and eager for a successful treasure hunt, they were surprised and disappointed to find little that would provoke a feeding frenzy at a trade show or auction. One, when pressed by a colleague for a report on the collection, even declared, in tones of appalled incredulity, "Why, there's nothing there!" Relative to expectations, there is indeed little here to satisfy the lusts and hungers of today's daguerreotype mavens. The collection boasts only one portrait of an African American woman; nine postmortems, most of them babies; eight depictions of animals (five dogs, two horses, and one cat drinking milk); sixteen occupationals, mostly military; three landscapes and seven waterscapes, many of them Niagara Falls concession views; eight architectural studies; eleven stereo-format images; twenty-eight daguerreotypes of drawings and paintings; twenty pieces of jewelry; and fifty-two other examples classifiable as unusual or exceptional. To these 163 items may be added another hundred that might be deemed desirable on today's collecting market. Surprisingly, what Horblit did acquire in great numbers was exactly that type of imagery against which the unusual is judged—that is, anonymous, convention-bound, formal studio portraiture.

Almost immediately, questions were raised about Horblit's collecting wisdom and about the quality not just of his daguerreotypes but of his collection as a whole. How could Horblit have justified buying so many daguerreotypes of such low value? How could he

FIGURE 14. "Family Daguerreotypes, found every where" from *Harper's New Monthly Magazine* 15, no. 86 (July 1857): 285; volume: 25.3 x 16.9 cm.

FIGURE 15.   Edward M. Tyler & Co. *Grandma Robinson*. Ninth plate daguerreotype.

have neglected to acquire more images of greater value? Had he lacked an "eye" for the daguerreotype? Had he been a collector of the "bottom-feeding" variety? What had he been trying to accomplish, if anything? All of these questions and others that have circulated must be answered accurately if a proper understanding of Horblit's genuine achievement as a collector is to be reached.

Regrettably, Horblit's untimely passing in 1988 robbed us of the opportunity to hear firsthand his answers to these questions. The answers must therefore be extrapolated from anecdote and from the collection itself. We do know something about how the collection was acquired. From the earliest development of an international art market for fine, rare, and historically important photography in the late 1960s, Horblit was on the mailing lists of all the major auction houses whose sales featured photographs. He also received catalogues from dealers specializing in photographica, and for any general auctions of Americana in which nineteenth-century photography might be included. He was thus well aware of the range of material on the market in both the United States and England, and of the prices being asked and realized for various items. Many of his paper photograph and album acquisitions were made at New York or London auctions. He faithfully annotated his catalogues, indicating the lots he bid on and the hammer prices. These notations sug-

GRANT B. ROMER

gest that he made relatively few purchases of daguerreotypes at auction. When he did buy, before 1980, it was almost always a framed English or French plate of large format; his winning bids on such lots were generally close to the low estimate. At the same auctions, unusual daguerreotypes carrying high estimates were also offered, but Horblit rarely pursued these. The largest grouping of daguerreotypes he acquired at auction was the remnant of the Josephine Cobb Collection, sold at an Americana auction house in Connecticut after the collector who had bought the collection entire skimmed off the finest and most valuable pieces for himself. No doubt attracted by the reputation of Ms. Cobb, who was renowned as a discerning pioneer collector of the daguerreotype, Horblit may have been unaware of the despoiled nature of the offering; he bought all of the multiple lots. Then again, the knowledge might have made little difference to him: there is no evidence that he ever attempted to ferret out other well-known collectors in order to acquire their collections or even learn of their contents.

The majority of Horblit's daguerreotypes are American and were purchased after 1980 from American dealers in early photography, all operating within the area where Horblit resided. He appreciated the personal service of dealers and was not a haunter of antique shops, flea markets, or the trade shows where many daguerreotypes were to be found. Dealers consulted about Horblit's interests have indicated that it was hard to sell high-priced individual pieces to him; he readily looked at such offerings, and admired their qualities, but in most instances declined to purchase them. He requested instead that groups be assembled by plate format—ten whole plates, for example, or twenty half plates —for his selection. He preferred images to be in intact cases, neither missing covers nor badly worn. When such lots were produced, he would offer to buy the entire set on a pre-determined, fixed-price basis: $500 for whole plates, $50 for halves, $25 for quarters, and $10 for sixths. He was indifferent to arguments as to the individual merits and variant values of each. Eventually, the dealers learned to eliminate from their lots material that exceeded Horblit's scale limits, contenting themselves with bulk sales of such hard-to-move items as leftovers from skimmed collections. After a number of modest acquisitions, Horblit purchased a lot of one thousand daguerreotypes assembled especially for him; the dealer who sold it to him characterized its contents as including "some decent stuff." That Horblit's acquisitions were edited in advance by dealers goes some way toward explaining the general blandness, at least by contemporary collecting standards, of his holdings.

To these bulk acquisitions he carefully added discrete items and groupings that rounded out his collection. Virtually every standard size and presentation mode is represented in quantity, along with some more unusual objects such as an example of a "mammoth" plate, an assortment of jewelry mounts, a box with a daguerreotype mounted to its lid, and a unique portrait of a stonemason mounted on a worked piece of marble. A range of daguerreotypes identified by maker (many by notable and well-regarded studios, as well as some by rarely encountered or unknown photographers) also made their way into Horblit's collection.

Had he wished to, Horblit would have been unable to acquire examples of Daguerre's own work because none came onto the market during his collecting lifetime (nor has any done so since). Only slightly less rare were the exploratory images made by the very first practitioners of the daguerreotype, such as Samuel Bemis; Horblit's acquisition of one whole plate view of 1840 by Bemis gives evidence of the attraction that such works held for him. He purchased early manuscript and published accounts of the process and no less than three copies of Daguerre's manual of 1839, along with various related scientific texts. The numerous copies of paintings and prints included in the collection may also reflect Horblit's interests in the essential duplicative character of photographic technology, and its relationship to printing.

Horblit's collecting style was pioneering, and his tastes, too, ran to "firsts." He did not collect for monetary gain or to appropriate the value of the objects he gathered; rather, possessed of an "insatiable curiosity," as his wife has observed, he collected to please and educate himself, confident that what he acquired would also help others to learn. His collecting logic, at least in regard to the daguerreotype, led him to assemble a historical representation of that process, the first truly commercially viable system of photography and the impetus for the first international photographic industry, primarily through its application to portraiture. While other collectors of similar rank focused on artistically unusual, or "masterpiece" daguerreotypes, Horblit was concerned with the form itself as an exemplar of photographic history. Of his collecting contemporaries, only Floyd and Marion Rinhart made a similar attempt to cover the broad range of the daguerreotype in their compilation. Over many years of acquisition and research, they developed a particularly strong belief in the validity of their endeavor, seemingly in defensive response to the differing tastes of other historians. Their sensitivity over the general neglect of the representative, characteristic manifestation of the daguerreotype is best expressed in their important work *The American Daguerreotype*, published in 1980, the same year that Horblit himself began actively to acquire daguerreotypes:

> Every daguerreotype has a place in the history of photography; the daguerreian art and its diversification can be better understood in a study comprising a wide range of specimens. . . . The daguerreotypes selected to illustrate this volume have been chosen to show a wide spectrum, from poor to excellent, rather than "prize winning" specimens. The illustrations are to instruct and not to entertain.[1]

FIGURE 16.   Photographer unknown. *Portrait of a Woman and Man, Seated and Holding Hands.*
Half plate daguerreotype.

These comments evidently constituted a pointed, if implicit, criticism of Beaumont Newhall's *The Daguerreotype in America*, initially published in 1960. The first extensively illustrated, process-specific history of photography, Newhall's book featured the type of imagery most commonly valued today—scenes, celebrities, occupationals, and so on—and did much to popularize and promote the collecting of daguerreotypes. Horblit owned a copy and surely studied it, though he did not adopt a Newhallian approach to collecting; neither did he, however, become interested in detailing his collection, as the Rinharts did, with examples demonstrating the minutiae of technical, commercial, and social daguerreian practice.

The influence of the legendary collector Sir Thomas Phillipps contributed much to the distinctive individuality and scope of Horblit's daguerreotype collection. Horblit began collecting Phillipps material in the late 1940s and continued to do so until he had become a "major purchaser of material relating to Phillipps himself and his printing and photographic activities;"[2] not coincidentally, Phillipps's photographic holdings became the nucleus of Horblit's own. Celebrated in the book world as perhaps the world's greatest book collector, Phillipps is by contrast virtually unknown to the average scholar or collector of photography. Horblit, himself often described as one of the great book collectors of the twentieth century,[3] certainly admired Phillipps's achievement, if not his personality: at the time of the centenary of Sir Thomas's death, Horblit remarked of him, "Fanatic, yes, but he salvaged heaven knows how much that would otherwise have been lost."[4] If Horblit himself could not be called a fanatic, he was nonetheless said to have been bitten by the "Phillipps bug." Eugenia Parry Janis, in her introduction to the catalogue of the posthumous exhibition of selections from Horblit's collection, postulated that he had found inspiration in Phillipps's "rabid curiosity and brute intelligence."[5]

In 1869, Phillipps wrote, "I am buying books because I wish to have one copy of every book in the world." Earlier he had provided a more reasoned explanation of his collecting purpose:

> In amassing my collection, I commenced purchasing everything that lay within my reach, to which I was instigated by reading various accounts of the destruction of valuable manuscripts. . . . I had not the ability to select, nor the resolution to let anything escape because it was of too trifling value. . . . As I advanced, the ardor of the pursuit increased until at last I became a perfect vello-maniac, and gave any price that was asked. Nor do I regret it, for my object was not only to secure good manuscripts for myself but also to raise public estimation of them, and consequently [to ensure that] more manuscripts [were] preserved.[6]

GRANT B. ROMER

Horblit knew these words and may well have adopted a similar approach to early photography, particularly the more "generic" material then being neglected by collectors of importance. While not a "daguerreo-maniac" ready to pay any price asked, he did jokingly express to one dealer his desire to "own them all." Not yet having developed his own "ability to select," Horblit may, like Phillipps, have resolved to salvage whatever "lay within . . . reach," no matter how "trifling." No other form of photography's first fifteen years could be acquired in such great numbers at such low cost. Whereas later photographs of similar sort might never assume any great value, those early photographs, in the fullness of time, would surely take on a worth similar to that accorded the first examples of printing using movable type. They were, in that one sense at least, singular.

There is evidence that the daguerreotype "object" held special appeal for Horblit. One dealer recounts that after he showed him how to refurbish worn and soiled cases, Harrison spent much time "rubbing each case with shoe polish and rag," as the dealer had shown him to do. His curiosity was also piqued by the hidden interiors of cases and frames, which he searched for inscriptions and enclosures. Taken though Horblit may have been with the material nature of the daguerreotype, however, we know nothing of what his reactions were to the actual imagery. Daguerreotype collectors typically have deep attachments to certain items in their collections; all have favorites before which they fall, bewitched, into trancelike contemplation. Which of Horblit's pieces held him in thrall is nowhere recorded. Avid collectors believe that the daguerreotype stands alone, defying comparison with other forms of photography, constituting the most beautiful, most mysterious, most special of all photographic processes. Did Horblit agree with this assessment? As much as he enjoyed the dazzle of his daguerreotypes, he may have felt that their real interest was as artifacts of early photographic history, not as images. He may have looked at each only once or twice, and never again. It has even been suggested, in an attempt to explain the "mediocrity" of his daguerreotype collection, that he acquired so many "bland" examples the better to set off the superiority of his early paper holdings, his real love. Such uncharitable speculations, dismissable on many grounds, serve to underscore the low value placed on most daguerreian portraiture of the sort Horblit collected in such great numbers.

Why *any* photograph made before 1860 should not rank high in the estimation of scholars, curators, and collectors is a question of some importance. Of all such early photography, the so-called average or garden-variety daguerreotype has perhaps suffered the greatest disdain. At a recent trade fair hosted by the Daguerreian Society, for example, one dealer, when asked why so few of his images were selling, remarked, "Let's face it, most of this stuff is not worth looking at twice." That a specialist dealer in daguerreotypes

FIGURE 17.   American School. *Portrait of a Seated Woman and Man.* Half plate daguerreotype.

could voice such an opinion may at first seem shocking, but in fact it is a view shared by many of the leading arbiters of taste in the world of photographic history and collecting. How it came to be so is a fascinating story in itself, one that gives some insight into the uses to which photography has historically been put and the standards to which it continues to be held.

The daguerreotype was the first kind of photograph to be made in the millions, thanks precisely to the widespread desire and fondness for memorializing portraiture. In order to serve this industry efficiently, portraits were created in a few recognizable and ubiquitous styles, easily lampooned and derided by satirists and critics of the day. One contemporary cartoon in *Harper's New Monthly Magazine*, captioned "Family Daguerreotypes, found every where," (figure 14), shows typical portraits of "Grandpa and Grandma," "Ma and Pa before Marriage," "Ma and Pa after Marriage," "The Baby," and "Junior and Sis."[7] Equivalents of these groupings can be found in great numbers in Horblit's collection (figures 15–19). The redundancy of the personal portrait daguerreotype essentially reflects the redundancy of humanity, a subject that was no more appealing to contemplate then than it is now.

Those serving as portraitists to a class of humanity not considered special have seldom been held in high esteem in any era. Period commentary reveals an abundance of derision for such practitioners. Marcus Root, one of the most ambitious of daguerreotypists, summed up the general attitude toward his "lesser" brethren:

> Sun painting, I was mortified to find, was considered a merely mechanical process, which might be learned in a few weeks, by a person of the most ordinary capacity and attainment. . . . Its operants, with not very numerous exceptions, bore a reputation similar to that of those itinerant portrait-painters, who anticipate the death of their victim, by destroying every trait of "life-likeness" in the faces they "execute." . . . My ambition forbade my patiently being ranked among recognized imbeciles and incapables.[8]

Even in their own day, portrait daguerreotypes were more often than not found wanting in many aspects: most were judged unsatisfactory as likenesses, as artful compositions, or as technical exemplars. Many a sitter, displeased with his or her likeness, was heard to exclaim, "I never *did* like the daguerreotype!"[9] *The Illustrated London News* of August 19, 1843, reported that it was not uncommon for a subject, after receiving a daguerreotype, to "fall foul on it and denounce it with a vindictiveness unspeakably amusing." Typical complaints branded the portraits "mere trick" and "stuff" and "imposition," "unfit for any exhibition"—"black, dirty daubs," "coarse and vile," "old, ugly things that never smile," "whitened shadows," "pale ghosts," and "most poor, even to paltriness" (for a modern parallel, think of people's responses to their driver's-license or passport photographs). And even when the likeness was acceptable, the object itself was anything but convenient. In 1851, the editors of the *Daguerreian Journal* noted,

> In the early days of Daguerreotype, our readers will remember what fragile and unsatisfactory things sun portraits were; how they needed to be always kept snug in Morocco cases safe from the action of the sun and the air, and how the spectator was obliged, before he could catch the proper light and see the likeness at all, to turn and twist it, and look sidewise, and at every possible angle, and with every practicable species of squint and visual contortion, like a magpie peering into a marrow bone.[10]

Similarly, Nathaniel Hawthorne's *House of Seven Gables* (also published in 1851) has a character express her own objections to such portraits: "I don't much like pictures of that sort—they are so hard and stern: besides dodging away from the eye, and trying to escape altogether. They are conscious of looking unamiable, I suppose, and therefore hate to be seen."[11]

The values of the daguerreotypist's clientele were no less subject to scorn than his product. The format allowed a wider segment of society to avail itself of the opportunity for personal portraiture, and many felt that the wrong class of people were being encouraged to have their pictures made, debasing the genre's traditions and sullying the purity of what was considered the "looking-glass raised to its highest degree." "Dunces" were now offered the privilege once reserved for "heroes," Herman Melville observed. The pictures adorning the walls of a typical Daguerreian room showed "pussy parsons, brazen barristers, flashing fops, and bedizened belles,"[12] while the customers therein provided their own spectacle: "From the nature of [the daguerreotypist's] art, a single day may bring under his hand a host of persons, comprising almost every type or organization, the ignorant and stolid, the flippant and conceited, the fastidious, the difficult, etc."[13]

The most prideful members of the profession harbored contempt for their patrons, as the *Daguerreian Journal* noted (and, it seems, approved):

> Were it not for the enterprising few engaged, our art would sink into deep insignificance. . . . We look upon a person visiting a Daguerreian Artist's room for the purpose of obtaining a cheap picture, as one who thinks little of the art, and less of his friends. Often it is the case, that a gentleman calls upon an artist, and wants a likeness,—from his appearance the artist is led to suppose him a member of the first society; and this may really be the case. . . . The artist steps forward, show his many specimens and asks, what size will you have? The person thus addressed, looks in the glass, surveys himself, and with all the dignity imaginable, exclaims,—Ah, oh! a small size, common—it's only for a friend,—what a compliment for a friend,—Ha! I wonder who your friends are.[14]

Nor were the middle-class sitters the only offenders; even those members of the "First Society" who were willing to pay for the most expensive work frequently imposed limitations on the creativity of the "daguerreian artist." In 1854 one observer of the portrait-making process declared, "We do not like to see . . . fancy pictures . . . , it is not what the parent wants of the daughter, nor the wife of the husband, nor the brother of the sister, nor the lover of the beloved."[15] Given these many constraints, the celebrated daguerreotypist J. H. Fitzgibbon could not refrain from musing, "Is it then to be wondered at that we find so many awful, ghost-like looking shadows poured out upon the world . . . ? Not at all!"[16]

The daguerreotype portrait industry was itself built upon the foundations of a pre-existing trade in painted portrait miniatures. These latter, most intimate of images were inextricably linked with personal history, yet even the most precious "mementos of regard" would become objects of little regard under another generation's caretakership. Someone reaching maturity in the age of the photograph could, by the 1860s, look back upon the painted portrait miniature dismissively:

> When we remember the old style of portrait we were obliged to be contented with, the horrible limning a lover got of his mistress for five guineas; the old monthly nurses they made of our mothers; and the resplendent maiden aunts, with their gold chains, watch-

es, and frightful turbans; and the race of fathers we keep by us in old drawers, gentleman built up stiffly, and all alike in blue coats, and brass buttons, with huge towels around their necks by way of cravats; when we remember the art at the command of the middle classes not forty years since, we are deeply thankful for the kindness of Sol in taking up the pencil and giving us a glimpse of nature once more.[17]

Soon enough, however, the daguerreotype portrait miniature would itself come to be seen as archaic. In *Life on the Mississippi*, published in 1883, Mark Twain describes encountering among the banal contents of a "whatnot" cabinet an assortment of

> spread open daguerreotypes of dim children, parents, cousins, aunts, and friends, in all attitudes but customary ones. . . . All these vague figures lavishly chained and ringed—metal indicated and secured by stripes and splashes of vivid gold bronze, all of them too much combed; too much fixed up; and all of them uncomfortable in inflexible Sunday clothes of a pattern which the spectator cannot realize could ever have been in fashion, husband and wife generally grouped together—husband sitting, wife standing all these fading years.[18]

With time, though, the wheel of fashion turned again, and the daguerreotype portrait came back into vogue, particularly when divorced from any direct family association. By the beginning of the twentieth century, daguerreotype portraits of anonymous sitters had become "collectible" to those with a taste for quaint things of earlier days. One enthusiast wrote of "The Charming Daguerreotype" in 1904:

> Short of an artist's fine handiwork, there has never been any means of reproducing the human face which has had the charm of the daguerreotype. The term "photographic," which is commonly used to designate the limitations of a too hard manner of drawing or painting, cannot be applied to it; for the soft, luminous shadows, the melting flesh-tones, the reality of life, are such that they may well excite the admiration and envy of skillful portrait-painters. This has been fully realized by connoisseurs, who have included large collections of daguerreotypes among their *objets d'art*, and the appreciation has extended until now there is a general searching for good examples of the art.
>
> The collector concerns himself first of all with artistic qualities. He soon finds that there are not so many available portraits of celebrities as would be supposed, and *often as specimens of work these are poor*, and valuable only for the likeness. Though it might be thought that a number of pictures of quite unknown persons would be dull and monotonous, yet this is not at all the effect that a collection makes, even upon the minds of those who are unbiased by special enthusiasm. For not only has the daguerreotype in itself elements that are sufficiently strong to make it entirely desirable for its own sake, but there is also an astonishing variety in the subjects: there is no sameness of physiognomies, such as is

inevitable with retouched plates; and the individual charm or character of the sitter is presented in so unspoiled and unmodified a manner that one seems to be looking at reflections made permanent on tiny looking-glasses.

The practice was in its greatest popularity in the middle of the last century. This was the period of the crinoline and the poke-bonnet, of the picturesque high stock and quaint long coat. Though the fashion of clothes was then strangely ugly, yet this very oddity has an interest for us now. The worst modes of a tasteless era cannot disguise the strong, manly faces that appear above the awkward, ill-fitting garments. And how often, when a well-worn case is opened, it discloses a vision of sweet femininity, her parted hair smoothly arranged and drawn down over her ears, and in her soft, dove-like eyes a modest, demure expression which adds the last charm to her distinguished beauty! What a subtle fragrance of delicate sentiment lingers about her! It seems scarcely possible, so natural does she appear in all the grace of her youth, thrilling with hope and life, that the sitter may have been dead for half a century, or, if still living, is now a wrinkled dame, grandmother or great-aunt, as her fate has held.

Although the presentations of these fair and charming women are naturally the most pleasing of the daguerreotypes, yet the fidelity of reproduction seems equally fortunate and admirable when the rounded contours of early life have changed to the sterner outlines of middle years and the wrinkles of age. The characteristic faces of men in their prime, stout elderly matrons, and old gentlemen and gentlewomen who reflect the tastes of a still earlier date, sustain the interest of a collection.[19]

This modest admiration for and somewhat patronizing attitude toward portrait daguerreotypes persisted up until the time when Harrison Horblit began seriously collecting photography, by which point the entire medium was coming to be reevaluated. John Szarkowski, in his 1973 book *Looking at Photographs*, a guide to photographic appreciation, offered a historical perspective on an American sixth plate daguerreotype portrait of two unidentified women:

When Daguerre announced his great invention to the public in the summer of 1839, he explained how it worked but not really what it was for. The process was obviously a miracle of the age of science, and like any miracle it was self-justifying. Painters did say that it would be a great aid to art, and physicists said it would be a great aid to science, but the important thing, on which everyone agreed, was that it was astonishing. Pictures of exquisite perfection had been formed directly by the forces of nature.

What the daguerreotype was in fact used for was recording the faces of millions of people. Of the countless thousands of daguerreotypes that survive, not one in a hundred shows a building or a waterfall or a street scene; the rest is an endless parade of ancestors.

FIGURE 18.   American School. *Portrait of a Seated Baby*. Sixth plate daguerreotype.

Most of these people were, outside their own family circles, nearly as anonymous when alive as their portraits are now. Nevertheless it is interesting to consider the fact that after Daguerre every man's family acquired a visual past: a tangible link with the history of the species. It is unfortunate that the picture [of the two women] has been lost to its rightful heirs. Who would not feel better for having two women as handsome, strong, and proud as these in his past?

An original daguerreotype is a small picture, generally smaller than the palm of one's hand, and exists on a surface of highly polished silver. The image, though infinitely detailed and subtle, is elusive. The picture should be looked at with its case not fully opened, preferably in private and by lamplight, as one would approach a secret.[20]

In our own day, few have chosen to regard portrait daguerreotypes as anything more than little pictures, difficult to see, of unknown people of no social consequence. Some pleasure, it is true, may be had in speculating as to the character of the sitter on the basis of fashion or physiognomy, but only the peculiar optical and physical properties of a cased daguerreotype give these photographs any greater appeal to the collector of fine photographs than, say, an old yearbook picture. Quite possibly Horblit himself felt the same essential disdain for the imagery of the average portrait daguerreotype when he first began collecting photography, but as his insight into the genre developed, his appetite for acquisition grew. Anyone sharing Horblit's curiosity must, on examining his thousands of daguerreotypes, recognize what the nature of that insight was.

Daguerreotypes are indeed little pictures, and were deliberately intended to be so. The qualities of the process, the ability to render minute detail with infinitely delicate subtlety, made it especially well suited to miniature portraiture. Today we have lost our taste for small pictures and no longer appreciate "likenesses in little," but in this we differ from our predecessors in the period when the daguerreotype came into being. The miniature picture had its own place among art forms and its own highly evolved aesthetic, much valued by the most refined levels of society. A prize need not be awarded to every daguerreotype, but each nonetheless holds a prize for the receptive viewer, the viewer who is able to follow one daguerrean era writer's advice to take a loupe in hand, adjust the light, and focus on the faces depicted therein: "Before you is the reflection . . . with nothing before or behind or around you to attract the eye; then it is the man rises before you, then it is the soul sees the man himself, and until some heedless person calls you 'back to earth' you believe you are looking on a 'thing of life.'"[21]

No other photographic process can offer such an experience. A viewer whose mind and heart are open to these mementos of human regard, once cared for with a "gentleness known and prompted only by pure love or the warmest of friendship" (in the words of the famed Philadelphia daguerreotypist Marcus Root), will soon realize the profound worth of these paradigms of personal relevance. Whether poor likenesses or poor artwork, these photographs had and still have great worth in the simplest of human terms. At the end of the daguerreian era, Root summed up their intrinsic emotional worth:

> In the order of nature, families are dispersed, by death or other causes; friends are severed; and the "old familiar faces" are no longer seen in our daily haunts. By heliography, our loved ones, dead or distant; our friends and acquaintances, however far removed, are retained with daily or hourly vision. To what extent domestic and social sentiments are conserved and perpetuated by these "shadows" of the loved and valued originals, everyone may judge. . . . With these literal transcripts of features and forms, once dear to us, ever at hand we are scarcely more likely to forget, or grow cold to their originals, than we should be in their corporeal presence. How can we exaggerate the value of an art which produces effects like these?[22]

As objects, daguerreotypes are indisputably difficult to look at, at least compared with conventional paper photographs. That difficulty is not, however, great, and it may be easily overcome given a little knowledge of the character of the optical properties of the image. Moreover, the slight extra effort needed to view a daguerreotype at maximum effect affords a visual reward unmatched by any other imaging system known. One experiences not an illuminated but rather a *luminous* image, seemingly shining with its own light. No less a celestial intimate than Sir John Herschel once observed that the daguerreotype to the talbotype was as the "sun compared to the moon." The illusion of light, air, and substance produced by mirror and mercury dissolves all picture-plane perception, giving the impression that the visual distance created is between viewer and subject, not between viewer and print surface.

Horblit also collected other examples of miniature portrait photography, including ivorytypes and cartes-de-visite; surely he perceived that the history of the photographic portrait miniature was yet to be written, and that when it was, it must begin with the daguerreotype.

Complex and multifaceted though they may be as a genre, individual daguerreotype portraits can seem either uniquely fascinating or redundantly dull, depending on the viewer's attitude. It is precisely this paradox that makes it difficult to work out the place of such portraits in the history of photography: they were so consciously calculated to answer basic human needs that they cannot be disassociated from the humanity they depict. They are like mankind itself, which, as Ishmael notes in Melville's *Moby-Dick*, has a dichotomous value: "Seat thyself sultanically among the moons of Saturn, and take high abstracted man alone; and he seems a wonder, a grandeur and a woe. But from the same point of view, take mankind in mass, and for the most part, they seem a mob of unnecessary duplicates, both contemporary and hereditary."[23]

Horblit, famed for his curiosity, sitting alone in his basement storage vault and looking over each of his daguerreotypes intensely, no doubt discovered such truths for himself. He knew that the daguerreotypes he had gathered were the most enigmatic of all the photographic objects within his collection—at once attractive and repulsive, infinitely varied and alike, wonderful and terrible, artful and artless, singular and common within the history of the medium. Certainly he found them fascinating, puzzling, and perhaps confounding. Unable to choose among them, he gave them all a place, if not a prize, confident that the passage of time would make them all the more interesting.

We may be assured that time will continue to influence changes in the future valuation of these photographs. The same forces that transformed now anonymous Egyptian funerary portraits by provincial artists into some of the most treasured and meaningful artifacts of human history can be expected to play upon daguerreotypes. As one millennium closes and another opens, then, these "ghostlike" images will begin to take on a radiant

FIGURE 19.   American School. *Portrait of a Seated Man Resting His Arm next to a Book.*
Half plate daguerreotype.

new life, representative of things that cannot yet be seen or felt by people of our own day. Magnified rather than diminished by temporal distance, these primal portraits made by a primal imaging system will be seen as artifacts of a technological Ur far beyond living memory. Every depicted being will be deemed a successful bidder for visual immortality, for that virtual life which this time-stopping technology promised to deliver to photography's first subjects. The vapors of death will evaporate from them, a sweet resurrection is assured.

GRANT B. ROMER

Systems of imaging yet to be invented will doubtless strive once again for the illusion of living presence that the daguerreotype so brilliantly conveys, and Horblit's collection of portrait daguerreotypes will be discovered anew by generations of scholars yet to come, luminologists of the genre. In the fullness of time, a better, more inclusive vision will evolve, unclouded by prejudice against little pictures or little people. Greater attention will be paid to variations in daguerreotypists' techniques and standards, more refined qualitative distinctions will be drawn, and a better perception of the palette of the daguerreotype process will be effected. The conventions of daguerreian portraiture will be thoroughly analyzed and compared with earlier and later portrait traditions, with the results enhancing the scholarly estimation of the achievement and importance of this imagery.

In Horblit's portrait daguerreotype collection, much grandeur can be found amid the blandeur. It is a true learning resource, of infinite value to those truly interested in the history of photography. Harrison Horblit's wisdom in acquiring "normal" examples of early photography will, I feel certain, be gratefully acknowledged by future generations of scholars unafflicted with the collecting myopia of our own time.

NOTES

1. Floyd and Marion Rinhart, *The American Daguerreotype* (Athens, Ga.: University of Georgia Press, 1981), xi.

2. G. Thomas Tarselle, "Harrison D. Horblit, Collector," *Gazette of the Grolier Club*, new ser., no. 48 (1997): 14.

3. Ibid., 5.

4. *New York Times*, Feb. 11, 1973, 63.

5. Louise Todd Ambler and Melissa Banta, eds., *The Invention of Photography and Its Impact on Learning* (Cambridge: Harvard University Library, 1989).

6. Seymour DeRicci, *English Collectors of Books and Manuscripts 1530–1930 and Their Marks of Ownership* (1930; facsimile reprint, New York: Burt Franklin, 1969), 119–20.

7. *Harper's New Monthly Magazine* 15, no. 86 (July 1857): 285–86.

8. Marcus Aurelius Root, *The Camera and the Pencil* (Philadelphia: J. B. Lippincott, 1864), xv.

9. Ibid., 93.

10. *The Daguerreian Journal* 2, no. 3 (June 16, 1851).

11. Nathaniel Hawthorne, *The House of Seven Gables* (1851; Bantam Classics, 1981), 68.

12. *Humphrey's Journal* 1, no. 4 (Jan. 1851): 155.

13. Root, *The Camera and the Pencil*, 38.

14. *The Daguerreian Journal* 2, no. 6 (Aug. 1851): 167.

15. Richard Rudisill, *Mirror Image: The Influence of the Daguerreotype on American Society* (Albuquerque: University of New Mexico Press, 1971), 215.

16. J. H. Fitzgibbon, "Daguerreotyping," *Western Journal and Civilian* (1851).

17. *The Photographic News*, Feb. 28, 1862, 185.

18. Mark Twain, *Life on the Mississippi* (1883; reprint, New York: Modern Library, 1994), 288.

19. Pauline King, "The Charming Daguerreotype," *Century Magazine* (1904): 81–82.

20. John Szarkowski, *Looking at Photographs* (New York: Museum of Modern Art, 1973), 11.

21. Rudisill, *Mirror Image*, 55n, 216.

22. Root, *The Camera and the Pencil*, xv.

23. Herman Melville, *Moby-Dick* (1851; reprint, New York: Bantam Classics, 1981), 428.

FIGURE 20.   British School. *James N. Merriman*, from the
Merriman Family Album (1852), leaf 30. Salted paper print; image:
14.1 x 11 cm., volume: 27.2 x 21.5 cm.

The Merriman Album

John Szarkowski

In the spirit of frank and full disclosure I should admit that I chose to address what I shall call the Merriman Album—out of all the riches of the Horblit collection—not only because it is an unfamiliar work of quality and charm, but because I thought it would be an easy subject. As the years pass, both the seductions of sloth and the mounting accumulation of unmet obligations propose such ignoble evasions. But the Calvinist in each of us will be reassured by the fact that I have been hoist with my own petard. The Merriman Album has proved, to me and to this point, a cryptogram without a key.

The album promised to be an easy game for at least four reasons. First, James Nathaniel Merriman (MA30, figure 20), whose picture appears on the title page of the album, was a younger member, and perhaps the last, of a long and distinguished line of apothecaries (not pharmacists, but in our terms general practitioners, approximately) who specialized as male midwives, or *accoucheurs*. His father's cousin's uncle, Samuel Merriman (1731–1818), the first of the line, was credited with attending either six thousand or ten thousand births.[1] (Even the smaller number is three times that claimed by William Carlos Williams.) Second, many of the subjects in the album are identified, more or less precisely, by name. These include a lord and two ladies, an admiral, a major, and a reverend. It seemed reasonable to hope that with these clues one might reconstitute, on paper, the community of one hundred souls or more who sat for this early and energetic photographer. Third, the album's putative date, 1852, places it at a moment when photography on paper was still a fairly uncommon activity. The ambition of this project, and the competence of its execution, strongly suggest an author who had made a serious effort to master the formidable technical demands of the craft, and who also gave no little thought to its pictorial possibilities. One would think that such a person—an amateur, surely, of the secure middle class, and one with available leisure—would have left a clear trail. Finally, to further narrow the research problem, it seemed likely that the pictures were made in Kensington, where Merriman resided.

Regrettably—and in spite of the generous help of many friends and colleagues who are much more knowledgeable than I in the field of early English photography—these promising clues have for the most part led only to further questions.[2] On the basis of supporting documentation, I can write only haltingly and tentatively about the subjects, and on the community that they formed, and must therefore accept the thankless task of addressing the pictures as pictures, to ask what evidence may be embedded in them.

To postpone, for a little, application to that hard duty, let me first review briefly the state of my objective knowledge, or ignorance, concerning the group that the album depicts. But even before that, the album itself should be approximately described. It contains eighty-one leaves, of which the last thirty-one are blank. One might describe the album as *small quarto*, but that term is not precisely appropriate, as is made clear by the number of leaves: obviously, no number of sheets folded twice (or *any* number of times) will produce a volume of eighty-one leaves. The mathematics are confirmed by the fact that the leaves are of at least three colors and weights. Out of cowardice, I did not ask the Houghton Library if I might disassemble the album to study its construction. Ms. Julie Mellby[3] tells me, however, that the album is typical of the commercially sold scrapbooks or albums of the period. A single sheet was folded over three quarters of an inch or so at the spine to allow an unoccupied space between leaves that would be later filled by the clippings or photos pasted into the album.

The first fifty leaves of the album hold 130 prints, ranging in size from about 2½ by 3¼ inches to 5¼ by 6½ inches. For the most part, they appear to me to be salt prints from calotype negatives, but I have been wrong in the past in my identification of photographic media and expect to be wrong again. Mr. R. Derek Wood has suggested that by 1852 most British photographers were in fact using collodion on glass and calling their pictures calotypes, presumably to separate themselves from the new commercial workers.[4] I like the idea, but the pictures nevertheless look to me like prints made from paper negatives.[5] Toward the end of the album there are a few prints that might be salt prints from glass plates. These pictures are also distinctive pictorially, which issue will be addressed later. Robert Hershkowitz, who has not seen the Merriman Album, has suggested that such a mix would be consonant with that seen in the famous Vacquerie Album of Victor Hugo and his circle, also dated 1852.[6]

The Merriman Album was sold to Harrison Horblit by Hans P. Kraus, Jr., who acquired it at auction from the Christie's South Kensington sale of March 29, 1984.[7] The consignor was June Stevens of Essex, who has kindly written me to say that neither she nor her husband can remember where they purchased the album.[8]

The author of the Christie's catalog entry, possibly Lindsey Stewart, states of the pictures that "most are captioned in pencil in a later hand,"[9] but gives no hint as to whether this judgment—the claim that the captions were added sometime after the album was assembled—was based on the style of penmanship or on evidence of another sort. The hand in which the captions are written is very different than that of the inscription on the title page, which bears the legend—in a self-consciously ornamented style, with each letter independent—"From E M I L Y to J.N.M., 21st SEPTEMBER, 1852" (MA1). But

JOHN SZARKOWSKI

though the writing style of the title page bears no resemblance to that of the captions, this does not seem to prove a great deal. It seems very likely that the writer of the title page did not normally make so painful an effort to convert her script into art.

The captioning of the album constitutes an interesting logic puzzle, which, I am confident, will be easily solved by some clear, untroubled mind. More than half of the people photographed in the album are identified, with widely varying degrees of precision. Some sitters are identified only as (for example) Mr. Westmore, or Mrs. Anterac, which might be thought typical of an adult thinking back to her (or conceivably his) childhood, when adults would not have been called by their first names, except close family relations, where the first name would be preceded by the name of the office—for instance, Aunt Georgie.

The prints in the album are embellished by a simple linear frame, drawn first in pencil, and then, in the first thirty-one leaves, overdrawn in ink (MA5b; figure 21). The pictures on the next twenty pages are outlined in pencil only. I am not prepared to guess how much time this sequence of decisions might require: from reversible ornamentation, to irreversible ornamentation, and then to the abandonment of the whole idea. But I suppose that the entire framing business might have spanned no more than one rainy weekend.

More to the point is the apparent fact that the identifying captions were written after the frames were drawn. The pencil or ink frames seem quite consistently to serve as the baseline for the caption writer.[10] It would also seem that on the first thirty-one sheets the graphite of the caption lies on top of the ink when the dependent part of a letter descends below the line.

According to the physical evidence only, the captions might have followed soon after the assembling of the album, but this possibility seems to be eliminated by historical considerations. Our curiosity in regard to the captions is piqued on page 3 of the album, on which a girl of perhaps seven or eight years is identified as *Aunt Georgie*. In the days when large families were commonplace, it was not very unusual to have aunts and uncles no older than oneself. Even then, however, it would be unusual to have an aunt who was quite substantially *younger* than her niece or nephew. Thus, either the captioning of the album was entrusted to a child—a child with a remarkably firm and confident hand—or the captions were indeed added at a later date, as proposed by the author of the Christie's catalog entry.

It may even be possible to identify the caption writer—at least by title—if one is allowed one crucial assumption. On page 2 of the album is a print identified as *Mrs. James Merriman and Family*. It shows a woman and four children—two girls and two boys. The same woman is identified on page 45 as *Grandmama*, and the younger girl in the family picture is the same as the child identified on page 3 as *Aunt Georgie*. The two boys seem to be those identified elsewhere as *Uncle Lenden* and *Uncle Harvey*.[11] Thus, if the photograph includes all the children of the family, the caption writer can only be the daughter or son of the older girl in the picture, elsewhere identified as *Minnie Merriman*. I have not yet found her married name.

The date of the album is relatively secure; or rather, a date for the album is secure, for it is not clear whether the inscription on the first page of the album—*From Emily to J.N.M. 21st September, 1852*—memorializes the gift of an empty album or a full one. Surely not altogether empty, for the inscription page includes a photograph of Merriman, which was clearly considered as an element in the design of the page. On the other hand, it seems unlikely that the album was full at this date. The sitters that I have proposed as the younger children of James Merriman—Georgianna, Lenden, and Harvey—seem older at the end of the album than at its start; as a guess, let us say two years older. It is my impression that the album was not gradually abandoned by a flagging interest, but rather pursued with vigor and attention up to the point where it was suddenly stopped, as by an exterior event. The sudden death of James Merriman late in 1854, from pneumonia, at the age of forty-eight, could have been such an event.

Merriman's death, at least approximately coincidental with the abandonment of the album, suggests the possibility that he was the photographer. But the disruption and shock that would have followed the unexpected death of the vigorous, middle-aged head of a lively family would probably have ended the game regardless of who the photographer was.

Merriman's claim to be named as the maker of these photographs is as good as the next person's, but not perceptibly better. He presumably had the means and the leisure to pursue what was then a demanding diversion, and Roger Taylor has correctly pointed out that, as an apothecary, he would have had a basic understanding of the chemical principles on which photography depended.[12] But in fact photography had already been invented; one did not need an understanding of photographic chemistry, one needed only to follow directions. At this stage, Merriman's candidacy as the mystery photographer might be addressed as fruitfully on the ground of intuitive psychology as on that of scholarship. The test is the portrait of Merriman reproduced here as figure 20 (MA30). Is this a self-portrait? Merriman is dressed in what, in mid-nineteenth-century middle-class England, might have been the equivalent of a National Guard officer's uniform. He appears to be in robust good health and excellent high spirits. He appears, in fact, to be in higher spirits than is commonly the case with the subjects of self-portraits. Self-portraits, on average, tend to be serious, even solemn, and they almost never suggest a genuine and pleasurable

FIGURE 21. British School. *Mr. and Mrs. Thompson*, from the *Merriman Family Album* (1852), leaf 5. Salted paper print; image: 14.1 x 11 cm., volume: 27.2 x 21.5 cm.

communication between the pictured and the picture-maker. In the case of the James Merriman portrait, I would guess that there was someone else in the room with him. Surely it is only in the past generation, since television achieved its hegemony, that we have developed a race of people who are able to smile sincerely and winningly into an un-attended camera lens.

Such speculation, based on the flimsiest of impressionistic testimony, should not, of course, be taken seriously, except as an indication of how a serious scholar can be driven to desperate speculation when deprived of facts.

Among the other possible suspects for the role of photographer is Emily, the woman who inscribed the album to Merriman. I have secretly rooted for Emily and have perhaps subconsciously dreamed that I might have a modest role in bringing to light still one more notable Victorian woman photographer. It seemed suggestive to me that no subject in the album was identified by the name Emily, and it seemed not impossible that she might be not only the photographer but a person of special, unrecorded importance in Merriman's too-brief life. She might, I reasoned, have withheld her own likeness from this visual census of the Merriman circle, in order that it might be remembered by Merriman with that sharper clarity—that truer drawing—that is preserved only in the cabinet of memory.

Alternatively, Emily might have been any of the several women who are unidentified in the album. Or she might have been any one of those who are identified only by title and last name. She might have been *Miss Turnley* (MA24t), or *Mrs. Barlow* (MA4b; figure 22), or even one of the daughters of *Lady Caroline Lascelles* (MA8t; figure 23). But Lady Caroline, who had ten children, named none of her seven daughters Emily.

Or, most likely, Emily was James Merriman's wife, in which case the caption writer, whom we have tentatively identified as her granddaughter, would likely not have called her Emily.

Other candidates are almost without number, but there are three names among the penciled captions in the album that require some special attention: the Mr. Price of *Mr. and Mrs. Price* (MA23b; figure 24) might possibly be William Lake Price (1810–1896), a pioneer in making photographs that attempted to finesse the awful factuality of the camera; but this work does not seem his cup of tea, and in any case it is thought that he did not begin making photographs until 1854.[13] Mr. Thompson of *Mr. and Mrs. Thompson* (MA5b) could be Charles Thurston Thompson, who would become the official photographer of the South Kensington Museum (later the Victoria and Albert). Four correspondents[14] have suggested the possibility that the subject of *Mr. Goodeve* (MA18, MA20) might be Thomas M. Goodeve, an early member of the Royal Photographic Society, who in 1852 exhibited photographic portraits made from the new collodion-on-glass (wet-plate) negatives, a method first published only the preceding year. If the prints in the Merriman Album are, as I believe, from paper negatives, it might make Goodeve seem a less likely candidate. I suspect that it was not common for a photographer to continue to make paper negatives after mastering the refractory wet-plate method; nevertheless, it was sometimes done. (In France, Gustave Le Gray continued to work in both media for years after photography on glass had become almost universal.)

If the Merriman Album is what it seems—an extended project that required a substantial investment of time and energy by both photographer and sitters, over a considerable period of time—then the photographer would almost surely have been either a member of the family or one so closely tied to it as to be essentially one of the group. I have discovered no such tie between Merriman and the photographers mentioned above.

A complete list of people who *might* have made these photographs would be, at this point, dishearteningly long, and composed primarily of names about which the history of photography knows little or nothing. However, before we turn away from the question of authorship, one more name, that of J. J. (John Jones) Merriman (born 1827), should be added to the list. J. J. Merriman was the author of *Notes on Kensington Square* (1887) and the maker of an album of photographic views of Kensington, thought to have been made in the 1860s.[15] I have been unable to discover a copy of *Notes* in this country and have not as yet been to London to see the album of photographs. J. J. Merriman was without doubt a conspicuous member of the extended Merriman family in question, since he was the only Merriman listed as a source for the *Dictionary of National Biography* articles on both Samuel I (1731–1818) and Samuel II (1771–1852). The latter article also refers to Samuel's first cousin John Merriman (1774–1839) and to his sons John (1800–1881) and James Nathaniel (1806–1854).

It is perhaps now time to approach what is perhaps the central question posed by the album: Who *are* these people?

As a first step, I tried to count them, but I have virtually no faith in the number I propose: 147. This figure is surely wrong, and possibly substantially wrong, since the faces and bodies of the people in the 129 prints are sometimes clear and sometimes vague. Many of the sitters are identified in terms that are not mutually exclusive; thus, we must guess as to whether *Uncle Merriman* on leaf MA12 is the same person as one of the many other male Merrimans who are there with a first name but a fading face.

Suffice it, for now, to say that the images of approximately 150 different people are included in the album. Of these, perhaps eighteen are identified as Merrimans, and approximately fifty as people with different surnames, of which an undetermined number might be Merriman women who have married, plus their families. Perhaps a third of the people in the album are unidentified. Many of these are children, and a dozen or so more are staff, of whom the caption writer might be expected to remember only those who later touched her (or his) own life. If the caption writer was the child of Minnie Merriman, as I have proposed, she (he) was not yet born when the last of the pictures were made.

The question of what we know about the people in the Merriman Album should perhaps be subdivided into two parts. The first half of the question is, What do we know of these people from the written record? and the second half is, What do we know about them from the photographs, which are of course the ultimate subject of our inquiry?

From the written record we know a good deal more than nothing, even if a great deal less than we would wish. Part of this information has already been conveyed, but this is an appropriate place to review the salient points. James Nathaniel Merriman, whose

Figure 22. British School. *Mr. and Mrs. James Barlow and Family,*
from the *Merriman Family Album* (1852), leaf 4. Salted paper print;
image: 9.7 x 11.4 cm., volume: 27.2 x 21.5 cm.

family is the nucleus around which the structure of this album revolves, is himself remembered chiefly as the son of his father, John (1774–1839), who, though himself a person of considerable stature, was remembered in large part as the cousin of Samuel (1771–1852), who was in turn junior to his uncle Samuel (1731–1818). To make things more complicated, the uncle of the younger Sam was also *his* father-in-law, since Samuel II married his cousin Ann. In addition to their normal Georgian and Victorian fecundity, it would seem that the Merrimans were quick to take on wards, who presumably were granted the family name.[16] All in all, the family is a subject that richly deserves the attention of a specialist; I can only hope that my errors will be relatively innocuous.

It is well documented that James Nathaniel Merriman was, like his older brother, John, and his father, John, an apothecary—that is, a general practitioner of medicine. In 1837, the year in which Victoria assumed her crown, John the father was appointed Apothecary Extraordinary to the Queen, and in the next year his sons John and James Nathaniel were also granted this office.[17] More precisely, the Merriman trio should perhaps be thought assigned to serve the queen's household at Kensington Palace, which

Victoria herself seemed to avoid, perhaps because it was the official residence of her mother, the Duchess of Kent. The duchess, like many mothers, had tried to persuade her daughter to trust her, and not to ask too many questions, but when at the age of eighteen Victoria acceded to the throne, she proved to be very much her own woman, and banished her mother's agents from her bedroom. From that time the queen and the most important members of her entourage stayed generally at Windsor or Osborne.[18] The Doctors Merriman were thus attached to a center of the monarch's authority, but a minor center, with power that was perhaps more apparent than real.

The duchess does not appear in the Merriman Album, but the man who was the comptroller of her household, Sir John Conroy (1786–1854), appears at least four times (MA38t; MA44, figure 25; MA46br; MA49).[19] Conroy might also be called the Duchess of Kent's secretary of state. His influence over the duchess had presumably been strengthened after her brother and adviser Leopold decided, in 1830, to accept an invitation to become King of Belgium, after which he felt obliged to spend most of his time in that country.

Conroy had represented the interests of the duchess (and perhaps his own) in the contest for the soul of Victoria, who, unless she died first, would be queen once the dissolute George IV (1762–1830) and the aging William IV (1765–1837) were out of the way. By the time the Merriman photographs were made, Conroy had long since failed the duchess in the task of preserving her hegemony over her daughter. He had apparently also lost a good deal of her money, and also of the queen's money, through bad, or unlucky, financial maneuvering.[20] There seems to be no evidence, however, that either the duchess or the queen was reduced to serious want.

Elizabeth Longford characterizes Conroy as a "man of extravagant ambitions, an intriguer, a vulgarian and a scamp. He had brains and like most villains he was not as black as he was painted."[21] She adds that "Conroy's manner, though overbearing, possessed a swashbuckling charm"; and speaking of a portrait painted by Fowler in 1827, she writes that "despite the thinning hair and the strangely cleft chin, there is a *panache* about the whole that must have had its effect."[22] The panache survives even photography's leveling gaze: if one was willing to follow anyone into the Valley of Death, or some similar place, on the strength of how authoritative he looked in a photograph, one might well follow the Conroy of figure 25. However, Sir John—also Colonel Conroy—never got to the Crimea, but died at home in 1854, the same year as James Nathaniel Merriman, when the war was in its second year.

Lady Caroline Lascelles also appears in the album, with three of her daughters (figure 23). Lady Caroline was one of the three celebrated Howard girls, her two younger sisters becoming Harriet, Countess Gower, and Georgianna, Lady Dover. I had hoped that Lady Caroline would supply a cornucopia of witty letters and diaries, with references to her visits to the Merriman place, and sharply etched caricatures of the principals. Alas, Lady Caroline's chief claim to literary immortality would seem to be as the preserver and transcriber of the letters of her two sisters, and in this project she advanced only through the letters of 1833, stopping almost two decades before she sat for the photographer of the Merriman Album.

Nevertheless, Lady Caroline, Sir John and Lady Conroy, and Admiral Deacon were all visitors to the Merriman house, and willing sitters for the unknown Merriman photographer. It seems clear that James N. Merriman's family was a family of some substance. It was not, of course, comparable in status to the great families of the new industrial and commercial middle classes, but it was a family that had risen to a level that mingled socially with the higher gentry, and even, on occasion, with the aristocracy.

The medical community was in 1852 still in the process of leaving the world of craftsmen, in which surgeon and barber had been the same person, and entering into the category of quasi-scientists and semi-intellectuals. The Merrimans and their circle are removed from us by only a century and a half, and they spoke a language that we might almost understand. We might even understand something about their social ambitions. Nevertheless, they are already in some ways strangers to us, and we should for that reason pay careful attention to them in these photographs, before the texture of their lives is lost altogether to our imagination.

This brings us to the pictures themselves. Unless they win our attention, whole archives of supporting data will not add much to their meaning.

Most of the pictures in the Merriman Album are carefully posed group portraits, including as many as nine sitters. (One photograph of the staff includes eleven people plus a dog, but the design of this picture is somewhat more mechanical than that of the others, perhaps because the servants were busier than the other sitters, and could not be expected to devote so much of their day to art.)

The informal group portrait—the conversation piece—perhaps embodied the greatest achievements of English painting before the nineteenth century. It is not easy to define with precision the distinction between the conversation piece and the model of group portraiture defined by Rembrandt and his Dutch followers; one might suggest, however, that the English version seems both more spontaneous in design and more frankly conventional in its concept. The typical conversation piece makes little effort to suggest a serious reason that the group in question is gathered together at the given place and time, except to have its picture painted. Nonetheless, many of these pictures have a charmingly unbut-

FIGURE 23. British School. *Lady Caroline Lascelles and Daughters*,
from the *Merriman Family Album* (1852), leaf 8. Salted paper print;
image: 9.6 x 11.9 cm., volume: 27.2 x 21.5 cm.

toned quality. E. D. H. Johnson claims that the Georgian conversation piece "is analogous
to today's candid camera shot,"[23] and it is undeniable that a picture such as Joseph
Highmore's *Mr. Oldham and His Guests*, of circa 1750, gives the impression of an invasion
of privacy with an immediacy matched by few photographs.

In my view, the maker of the Merriman portraits has succeeded much better than
might reasonably be expected in translating at least some of the virtues of the English portrait tradition into the intractable medium of photography. In the best of the pictures, the
composition is both stable and graceful, and the sitters are clearly drawn, well lighted, and
seemingly alert and at ease. Those prints that seem unfaded (or only slightly faded) show
us the sitters in a space that is coherent and persuasive, without unexplained holes or
patches.

Like many early photographic portraits, most of the Merriman pictures were made
in an outdoor studio, dressed up with screens, rugs, and furniture to resemble an interior.
It seems likely that the studio was on a shadowed side of the house, since none of the pic-

FIGURE 24.   British School. *Mr. and Mrs. Price*, from the *Merriman Family Album* (1852), leaf 23. Salted paper print; image: 9.6 x 12 cm., volume: 27.2 x 21.5 cm.

tures made in it shows direct sunlight. In this sense the Merriman pictures are unlike the portraits that David Octavius Hill and Robert Adamson had made a few years earlier. As a painter, Hill was enamored of the strong chiaroscuro effects most famously associated with Rembrandt, and many of the most impressive photographic portraits made by him and Adamson are blocked out with a strong, simple pattern of bright sunlight and deep shadow. The light in the Merriman pictures is in comparison modulated and enveloping, and insinuates itself into areas that Hill would have rendered as black. Hill's fondness for dramatic lighting is perhaps something of an anomaly in British art, which characteristically prefers in painting the same objective, watery light that most often falls on those northern islands.

The problem of portrait photography is as much psychological as it is technical or formal. The beauty of the design and the lighting, and the gorgeous description of surfaces, will not count for much if the subject appears to wish fervently that he or she were elsewhere. The best portrait photographers—such as Nadar, and Stieglitz, and Irving Penn—somehow persuade their sitters that together they are engaged in an exploration that is important and potentially wonderful. Those who have tried their hand at photographic group portraits know that the chances of succeeding in this act of bewitchment decrease more or less exponentially with the number of sitters.[24] The Merriman photographer has been remarkably successful with this very difficult problem. The photographer was of course aided by the fact that the subjects necessarily had to be at least relatively willing accomplices. Early photographers could not hope to catch their sitters unaware, and the fact that their cooperation was necessary made the undertaking something of a joint enterprise—perhaps in this case a kind of family game, but without the element of competition (at least not an *obvious* element of competition: one could not say that the affair was without its losers, among whom *Miss M. Hare* [MA37] may have counted herself). In addition to the fact that the sitters were willing collaborators, it is probably also true that in 1852 their experience with photography was very limited; they did not yet know how treacherously it might traduce them, adding years to their faces and unnatural bulges to their figures.

Shortly after inventing modern photography, William Henry Fox Talbot suggested some of the uses to which his invention might be applied. Photography could describe a specific object more precisely, or at least more persuasively, than any other picture-making system, and because of this ability it seemed to Talbot to offer an excellent method for producing a visual inventory of one's possessions. Talbot demonstrated his point by producing photographs of portions of his library, and his collections of porcelain and crystal, and Mrs. Talbot's hats. Within the limits of his method and his skill, these documents show exactly what an insurance adjuster would want to know: the facts, unobscured by poetic feeling, sentiment, or artistic ambition.

The maker of the Merriman pictures does not inventory the possessions of the house in the same way, but one might say that possessions form a parenthetical subtext in the Merriman portraits. The portraits were made, as noted, outdoors, in a partially protected court, in which screens and rugs and indoor furniture were arranged to suggest that the sitters were in fact inside, close to the hearth. One should also note that little effort was made to crop out the telltale edges of the pictures, which give the game away. Perhaps the exercise should be considered not as an ordinary deception, but as a play, a kind of entertainment, not really intended to be taken for the unvarnished truth.

In any case, it is interesting that the set is not static here, as we would expect it to be for substantial periods in the studio of a professional; on the contrary, it changes more or less continually. At least six different tables are used, with a wide variety of still-life objects on them, and all manner of chairs, but no pictures—perhaps the screens that played the part of walls were judged too precarious to bear their weight. As to whether this variety of apparatus was introduced for pictorial variety, or as an indication of material prosperity, or as an unexamined mixture of these sacred and profane motives, I have no idea.

⟶∍•⟨⟵

So, let us consider what we have in hand—not what we are lacking, but what we have. What we have is something very rare: a coherent body of pictures with no written commentary, no notes by the author, no self-serving clarification by the chief acolyte, no literary duel between competing critics. We have here an album of impressive early photographs that are almost unsullied by contemporary documentation, and innocent of interpretation. We have, therefore, an almost ideal subject, if we wish to study what kinds of meanings photographs might convey, in their own flesh, without reference to the pencil inscriptions on their backs.

At this point in my story—in early December 1997—I was informed by Mark Haworth-Booth that Carolyn Starren of the Kensington Library thought it likely that the Merriman Album recorded not the family and circle of James Nathaniel Merriman, apothecary from Kensington, but those of James Nathaniel Merriman, brewer from Marlborough, in Wiltshire. This question has not yet been resolved. I would at this juncture still cast my vote for the apothecary from Kensington,[25] but I would not bet a significant sum on the matter. The essential point is that the photographs will not answer the question for us.

So what do these pictures tell us?

They tell us very little that will stand as hard evidence. But let us remind ourselves that they are after all only pictures; we know that we cannot expect pictures to prove the truth of Christian doctrine, or even its falseness; or the superiority of socialism (or capitalism) as an economic system; or the honorableness or the baseness of the person in a portrait. Pictures are able to tell us little beyond the realm of appearances, discovered or invented.

One thing that the photographs tell us about the Merriman circle is that its members were well and expensively dressed. I am not an expert on fashion, but it seems to me that most of the adults in the Merriman Album, excepting servants, have paid much more than perfunctory attention to their clothes. An exception might possibly be made of Lady Caroline Lascelles, who, since she is presumably the social superior of almost everyone else in the circle, is able to dress not dowdily, but with what we might call disinterested understatement. The state of these people's wardrobes is surely less important than the state of their souls, but their wardrobes are more visible, and they tell us that these are people who have high expectations of themselves, and of whom we are also expected to expect much.

JOHN SZARKOWSKI

FIGURE 25. British School. *Sir John Conroy*, from the *Merriman Family Album* (1852), leaf 44. Salted paper print; image: 14.2 x 10 cm., volume: 27.2 x 21.5 cm.

FIGURE 26.   British School. *Family Group*, from the *Merriman Family Album* (1852), leaf 51.
Salted paper print; image: 13.8 x 16.8 cm., volume: 27.2 x 21.5 cm.

The pictures cannot tell us that these people love each other, but the preponderance
of family groups demonstrates that the family is central to their sense of who they are. For
the greater part, it would seem that the pictures with only one sitter are of people without
family, or with no family present. The pictures also tell us that both the photographer and
his sitters knew something of the tradition of British portraiture, and lent themselves to
the project of producing a body of photographs that would extend, however modestly, that
tradition for their own family and circle. It is clear that the photographer is working from
a well-established model. I do not mean that the photographer is posing his models while

holding in his hand an engraving after some dead painter; I mean rather that he or she has absorbed a generalized notion of a proper style for familial group portraiture, both from prints and from access to pictures in houses of substance. In the days before photo-mechanical reproduction, it seems to me likely that for the Merriman photographer such an abstract ideal of portraiture would be defined in terms of the masters of the eighteenth century—Gainsborough and even Hogarth—rather than the recent, flashier example of painters such as Henry Raeburn and Thomas Lawrence, who did not die until J. N. Merriman had attained his full height.

It is true, of course, that unless great pains are taken to subvert its natural tendencies, photography will take delight in fact, and will thus seem, on the surface, closer to Hogarth than to Raeburn. Not too much should be made of this; but it is surely not going too far to point out that until the nineteenth century, English painting was predominantly portrait painting—the painting of likenesses—and that except during the time of van Dyck and the Tudor kings, the preferred manner for English portraits was unremittingly factual.[26]

One of the most interesting aspects of the Merriman Album does not appear until its very last leaves. On leaf 45 we see a picture of *Grandma and Aunt Georgie*, which has abandoned the tactic of constructing a picture according to the tradition of portrait painting, and instead adopts the basic tenet of modern photography: one edits the world by standing in the right place, and by intelligent framing, and by exposing the sensitive sheet at the right time. Again on leaves 50 and 51, the principle of the constructed *tableau*—the principle that informs the making of the pictures of the album until its last pages—is jettisoned, in favor of a new idea in which the subjects do not seem posed at all; or if they *are* posed, it is according to an unfamiliar principle of balance, which favors the provisional, the eccentric, the improvised.

Again, there are a dozen possible explanations for this sudden and dramatic change, of which the limiting cases might be, 1) that the original photographer suddenly changed his mind, or hers, concerning what an interesting photograph might look like; or 2) that some of the last pictures in the album were made by a different photographer.

It is worth noting that in the last picture in the album (MA51; figure 26) one can finally see and understand the area—behind the stairs—that had served as the outdoor studio, revealed now, without embarrassment, to be not a stage but an everyday part of a functional house.

Whatever the reasons for this change at the end of the Merriman Album, it anticipates dramatically the way in which radical nineteenth-century photography—that is, photography that was not handicapped by too solicitous a concern for accepted artistic virtues—revised our sense of pictorial possibilities. In this new and modern world, design, or the will to order, is no longer composition. It is not the construction of an omniscient and invisible inventor, but rather the record of what is seen from an unfamiliar point of view.

———⊰•⊱———

We are thus confronted with a hundred speculations. We have a fair-sized collection of facts, and precious little basis for judging what they mean. We can choose Door A or Door B, but each opens onto a hall with more doors, and even if we should guess right every time, how would we *know* we were right?

We know with moral certainty only that the Merriman pictures show us people who were once alive, each of whom was, however subtly, unique. The sitters present to us ungrudgingly, even eagerly, what they hope will be their best sides—the objective correlatives of the best aspects of their characters. We need know no more than this to find the pictures deeply absorbing. They are not answers, but questions. Not theories, but experience. They are evidence of a world that will not be enclosed within systems.

Afterword

In January 1998, shortly after sending the preceding essay to the Houghton Library, I received a letter forwarded by Mark Haworth-Booth, addressed to him by Carolyn Starren and accompanied by a half-pound packet of photocopies. The letter began: "Mark—I suddenly hit paydirt and have identified nearly all of the names." The documentation attached made it clear that the J. N. Merriman of the album was, in fact, the *accoucheur* from Kensington, not the brewer from Marlborough. It also identified Emily as Mrs. James Nathaniel Merriman, the former Emily Yorke Hutchins. In addition, it located the residences of many of the subjects of the album either on or near Kensington Square, putting to rest the conjecture (discussed above) that the photographs might have been made by Thomas M. Goodeve, since it was the *Joseph* Goodeves who were the Merrimans' neighbors on Kensington Square.

Ms. Starren's searches in the parish records of Saint Mary Abbots confirmed that the picture *Mrs. James Merriman and Family* does include all of the four surviving children: Emily Jane, Thomas Lenden, Harvey Henry, and Georgianna Marian. A fifth child, Henry John, died in infancy in 1839. Thus it would seem established that the captioning of the album was done by a child of the elder daughter of James Nathaniel and Emily.

A complication is added by the fact that the baptismal records identify the Merrimans' elder daughter as Emily Jane, not as Minnie; indeed, Ms. Starren could find no candidate for our Minnie Merriman before the twentieth century. We now know, however, that Mrs. Merriman was also named Emily, and since "minnie" was an informal synonym for "mother" in Scotland and northern England,[27] might it not also have been used as a nickname meaning "she with Mother's name"? Or possibly meaning "miniature," a smaller copy?

In any case, Carolyn Starren seems well on her way to producing a family tree for the Merriman clan, which will bring at least the genealogical mysteries to heel.

1. *The Dictionary of National Biography* 13 (1909), p. 293, favors the 10,000 figure; Brian Hill, in "All in the Family: Samuel Merriman and His Relations," *The Practitioner* 207 (July–December 1971), satisfies himself with "more than six thousand."

2. My friends and colleagues have been extraordinarily generous in contributing their knowledge, time, and energy to my study of the Merriman Album. Without them even the halting and tentative progress that I have made would have been impossible. Most especially, I must ackowledge the assistance of Catherine Bergin of the Wellcome Institute for the History of Medicine; Anne Hammond of *The History of Photography*; Mark Haworth-Booth of the Victoria and Albert Museum; Robert Hershkowitz; Hans P. Kraus, Jr.; Julie Mellby of the Houghton Library; Pam Roberts of the Royal Photographic Society; Larry J. Schaaf; Carolyn Starren of the Kensington Library; June Stevens; Lindsey S. Stewart of Christie's; Roger Taylor; and R. Derek Wood.

3. In conversation, October 1997. Julie Mellby is Assistant Curator in the Department of Printing and Graphic Arts at the Houghton Library. She has been of invaluable assistance in the research on which this paper is based.

4. Letter from R. Derek Wood to Anne Hammond, October 14, 1997, passed on to the author. In the letter Mr. Wood says, "I notice that the Christie's catalogue entry describes the Merriman Album as containing 'calotype' portraits. Of course I have to groan loudly here. Even from the two illustrations as seen on the photocopy of the Christie's entry it looks as if the resolution of the images [is] unlikely to have been obtained with paper negatives, but indeed there is no reason to suppose that most photographers in London in 1852 used anything other than Collodion glass negatives. It really is about time curators and collectors grew up in this respect. Even Talbot's sidekicks Henneman and Malone were using Archer's Collodion technique in 1852 (and earlier) and if they (and Talbot) wanted to call these Talbotypes or Calotypes then there is no excuse now to continue that nonsense." With all respect to Mr.

Wood, almost all the pictures in the Merriman Album still look to me like salt prints from paper negatives. In any case, we are dealing here, almost surely, with one, as yet unknown, amateur, and what "most photographers in London in 1852 used" is not really to the point.

5. Ibid. Wood thought that the pictures looked too sharp to be from a paper negative, but he was basing his opinion on a copy of a photomechanical reproduction, in which the dot pattern naturally increases the impression of sharpness.

6. Letter from Robert Hershkowitz to the author, July 29, 1997.

7. Hans P. Kraus, Jr., to the author, July 23, 1997.

8. June Stevens to the author, August 11, 1997.

9. Catalog entry for lot number 315, Christie's South Kensington, March 29, 1984.

10. Ms. Julie Mellby, who is much more familiar with mid-nineteenth-century albums (photographic and otherwise) than I, gave her independent opinion that the captions do use the linear frames as a baseline.

11. *Uncle Len* is identified on leaf 3, and he and *Uncle Harvey* appear on leaf 16, and again (a year or two later?) on leaf 50.

12. Letter from Roger Taylor to the author, August 21, 1997.

13. Helmut and Alison Gernsheim, *The History of Photography 1685–1914* (New York: McGraw-Hill, 1969), 245.

14. R. Derek Wood, Anne Hammond, Mark Haworth-Booth, and Roger Taylor.

15. The existence of the album of photographs, which I have not seen, was brought to my attention by R. Derek Wood. It is in the collection of the Local Studies Section of the Kensington Central Library, London W8 7RX.

16. Samuel Merriman (1771–1852) raised eight children, three of his own and five who were distant relations of his wife. From W. MacMichael, *Lives of British Physicians* (London: W. Legg and Company, 1887), 359.

17. A. M. Cooke, "Queen Victoria's Medical Household," *Medical History* 26 (1982): 315. It might also be pointed out here that "Apothecary

Extraordinary" seems to mean not an apothecary of extraordinary merit or authority, but rather something similar to "visiting professor."

18. Ibid., 26:307ff.

19. The pictures listed are captioned with Conroy's name (in MA46br he is identified as *Colonel Conroy*), but the picture of the man on the horse (MA46t) also seems to be Conroy, not the much younger Major Hammer.

20. Elizabeth Longford, *Victoria R.I.* (London: Weidenfeld and Nicolson, 1964), 35–36.

21. Ibid., 35.

22. Ibid., 38.

23. E. D. H. Johnson, *Paintings of the British Social Scene: From Hogarth to Sickert* (London, Weidenfeld and Nicolson, 1986), 46.

24. If one can hope for one good negative in five tries with a single sitter, then on a purely statistical basis one should make 625 exposures to get a good negative of four sitters in one picture. In practice, of course, success and even luck are not purely statistical matters: the circumstance that might persuade the first sitter to forget the pain of posing might also work for the second.

25. The presence of Sir John Conroy seems good evidence, and also that of the Reverend John Sperling, assuming that he was the Reverend John H. Sperling, who (I have been informed by R. Derek Wood) was curate of Kensington from 1849 to 1856.

26. The momentary success of the continental Van Dyck and his successors does not invalidate the main point. The Stuarts ruled England for almost as long as the Tudors, but after they were deposed, they and their papist ways were forgotten.

27. *Random House Dictionary of the English Language*, 2d ed.

ROMAN VIEWS

Andrew Szegedy-Maszak

The extraordinary collection of photographs compiled by Harrison Horblit contains numerous pictures of nineteenth century Rome. This essay will examine two sets of such images, long views of the city taken from Monte Pincio and more intimate studies of one of the best-preserved pagan temples, the so-called Temple of Vesta in the Forum Boarium.[1] Taken together, these images illustrate some of the most important concerns of both the photographers and their audience.

I

Before turning to the early photographs of Rome, we may glance back to the century before photography was invented, by which time the conventions of European travel were already well established. In considering the special fascination of the south, Dr. Johnson observed, "All our religion, all our arts, almost all that sets us above savages, has come from the shores of the Mediterranean." He concluded that familiarity with the region should be the "grand object of travel," and shortly before he died (without himself ever having visited Italy), poignantly declared, "A man who has not been to Italy is always conscious of an inferiority, from not having seen what it is expected a man should see." The cultural imperative to see what one *should* see was one of the foundations of the Grand Tour, the edifying itinerary that took the well-heeled and ostensibly well-read eighteenth-century British traveler to the most important sites in Europe.[2]

One of Dr. Johnson's contemporaries and friends was the indefatigable traveler and diarist Hester Thrale Piozzi. Stylistically, her account of her own Grand Tour may tend toward the breathless, but she was nonetheless a shrewd and open-eyed observer of her surroundings. In a typically underpunctuated journal entry, she noted, "Mrs. Miller has been in Italy too, & has written her travels; and brought home a fine Vase which once belonged I think she says either to Cicero or Virgil I forget which." Together Dr. Johnson and Mrs. Miller, as described by Mrs. Piozzi, neatly illustrate the primary impulses behind travel: the acquisition of "culture," the acquisition of goods (it was in the late eighteenth century that such objects first came to be called souvenirs), and the ability to tell others about one's experiences.

In the tradition of English travel, Rome was the end station on the Grand Tour, the goal that combined aesthetic, religious, and historic interest with the equally appealing opportunity to purchase antiquities and other works of art. The English presence was so strong, especially in the area around the Piazza di Spagna, as to reassure the less confident Anglophone tourist while also serving as a source of wry complaint for the more sophisticated visitor.

In the early nineteenth century, areas that had previously been accessible only to those of considerable means and leisure became available for exploration by a newly mobile middle class.[3] It was also at this time that Americans began to make the journey to Europe in ever-increasing numbers.[4] To accommodate the needs of such travelers, there developed an extensive industry that included railway, steamship, and carriage companies, hotels and restaurants, professional guide services, and, not least, commercial photographic studios that produced images of the "most extraordinary sites and monuments from the whole world."[5] Book publishers, too, took part in the boom, printing guidebooks in popular series such as Baedeker and Murray as well as thousands of titles by amateur traveler/authors.[6] Just as the latter half of the nineteenth century was a golden age of photographic innovation and exploration, it was also a great period of travel and travel narrative. Such texts range in tone from the didactic to the rhapsodic, but all display a remarkable uniformity in their attitude toward the foreign countries and cultures that are their subjects. The premise of this essay, simply put, is that photographs and narratives from this period share an audience, are controlled by similar conventions, and, in turn, reflect and reinforce a particular vision of Rome.

Most travelers had their eyes fixed firmly on the city's grand past, despite the fact that the mid-nineteenth century was a period of considerable turmoil in Italy, as it was elsewhere in Europe. Pope Pius IX, elected in 1846, began his reign with a series of popular reforms such as declaring amnesty for political prisoners, thereby raising hopes among liberal reformers, both Italian and foreign, that the papacy would participate in the establishment of a unified Italy. One can get a vivid sense of such expectations in the journals and journalism of the American expatriate Margaret Fuller. In May 1847 she wrote of the new pope,

> He is a man of noble and good aspect, who, it is easy to see, has set his heart upon doing something solid for the benefit of Man. . . . The Italians . . . deliver themselves, with all the vivacity of their temperament, to perpetual hurra [sic], vivas, rockets, and torch-light processions.[7]

Her comment about the vivacity of the Italian temperament sounds a note typical of northern travelers' attitudes toward the Italians they encountered.

ANDREW SZEGEDY-MASZAK

FIGURE 27.   Robert Macpherson. *View over Rome Taking in the Vatican, from Monte Pincio,*
between 1858 and 1868. Albumen silver print; image: 24.4 x 40.2 cm., mount: 45.5 x 60.5 cm.

If Fuller's interest in the Italian domestic politics of her day was unusual for a foreign visitor—and all the more so in that she supported the progressive Risorgimento—she
was much more conventional in her mistrust of the institutional Church. Within two
years, the Republicans would be defeated, though their campaign for a united Italy would
continue for another twenty years. In the meantime, the pope was to ally himself completely with the forces of reaction, fleeing to the kingdom of Naples and remaining in exile
there until his reinstatement by French troops in 1850. In her later letters, Fuller expressed
a deep regret at Pius's about-face, a regret that would eventually harden into a fierce anti-
clericalism and anti-Catholicism.[8] As we shall see, her hostility toward the Church was
distinctive largely for its intensity; the sentiment itself was amply echoed in the writings of
many other travelers from both England and America.

I have spent a little time on Margaret Fuller because she is a useful gauge for some
of the prevalent points of view held by Anglophone visitors to Rome.[9] Fuller herself lived
in Italy for several years, took an Italian husband and bore him a son, and appraised short-
term tourists with an almost gleeful contempt:

Many persons run about Rome for nine days and then go away; they might as well expect to see it so, as to appreciate the Venus by throwing a stone at it. . . . No: Rome is not a nine-days' wonder, and those who try to make it such lose the ideal Rome (if they ever had it) without gaining any notion of the real.[10]

Of course, the vast majority of foreigners still spent only the requisite nine days in the city, or perhaps slightly longer: under the heading "Duration of Visit," the Baedeker guidebook of 1881 advises a minimum stay of ten to fourteen days "even to obtain a hasty glimpse of the matchless attractions of Rome." Noting that the traveler must "economise time by drawing up a careful programme," Baedeker then offers a day-by-day listing of the chief sites, organized by location and calibrated from the more significant to the less.[11] The guidebook thus assists its reader in the main task of his or her journey—that is, going to see those things that, as Dr. Johnson said, one *should* see. In effect, the agenda set for a visitor to almost any place in the world is fundamentally a mimetic process in that it depends on reports from other visitors rather than on the interests of the local populace; whether it is the program outlined by Baedeker or the list of four-star attractions in a modern Blue Guide, such a carefully prescribed itinerary both orchestrates and validates the experience of the traveler.[12]

As I have already implied, one of the most striking features of travel narratives is how little attention they pay to the historical events unfolding at the time of their composition. For the authors of such accounts, contact with the "real" Rome that Fuller referred to was limited to hotels, restaurants, and shops; likewise, the Italians they met were largely service staff, including waiters, shopkeepers, carriage drivers, and professional guides.[13] The Eternal City, as defined by the guidebook, for the most part corresponded to Fuller's "ideal" Rome. It was to be appreciated primarily as an amalgam of great monuments—both ancient pagan ruins and grand Christian churches—along with galleries stocked with classical sculpture and Renaissance painting. To judge from their travel memoirs, the most pervasive literary influences on visitors' perceptions consisted of partially remembered classical texts (especially Vergil and Cicero), quotations from Byron (particularly the Roman sections of *Childe Harold*), and occasional allusions to Goethe and Chateaubriand. On the visual side, some travelers carried with them more or less vague memories of classicizing painting, notably Poussin and Claude, but many more had seen the widely distributed vedute by printmakers. The most famous views were those by Piranesi, though numerous other artists' works were also available at a government-sponsored shop near the Trevi Fountain. The printmakers' subjects, as described by the 1850 Murray's guidebook, comprised the "principal ancient and modern monuments within and without the city."[14]

FIGURE 28.   James Anderson. *View of the Cathedral of St. Peter and the Vatican, Taken from behind the Fountain of Monte Pincio*, 1860s. Albumen silver print; image: 25.4 x 34.6 cm., mount: 49.4 x 63.8 cm.

II

By 1856, Murray's guidebook could advise its readers, "Photography has been of late very successfully applied in delineating the monuments of ancient and modern Rome. By far the finest are those made by our countryman Mr. Macpherson."[15] In the first section of this essay, I have tried to sketch some of the most significant elements of the cultural context in which photographers began to depict the city of Rome.[16] I have concentrated on the foreign visitors because just as they had been the chief purchasers of the earlier drawn and printed views, they now constituted the primary audience for photographs. The choice of subject matter for this new medium replicated that for its predecessors, and in fact, some of the personnel even remained the same: several of the midcentury photographers, notably Tommaso Cuccioni, had begun their careers as engravers or publishers of engraved *vedute*. As a result, Roman photographic views from this period adhered to a canon not only of established sites but also of points of view from which those sites were to be captured.[17]

On his or her first full day in Rome, the tourist was sternly admonished by Baedeker to hire a carriage and make a rolling sweep past most of the major sites: "The first part of this [day] had better be devoted to what may be called an 'Orientation Drive.'"[18] Thereby the traveler would get a preliminary glimpse of each of the places to be visited individually later in the week. In addition, the orientation allowed the newly arrived visitor to draw in his or her mind the web of interrelations that defined, in Margaret Fuller's phrase, the ideal city. The best way to conclude the day, Baedeker advised, was with an evening spent on the Monte Pincio. This low hill, adjacent to the Piazza del Popolo and thus near the densest concentration of tourist hotels, then boasted the city's only fully public park, attractively landscaped with gardens, fountains, footpaths, and carriage roads; both Roman residents and foreign visitors congregated there to drive, to stroll, and to socialize. In other words, it was a place that charmingly combined the picturesque foreignness of Rome with a comfortable sense of being among one's own people, an ambience good-naturedly evoked by Henry James:

> Such a staring, lounging, dandified amiable crowd! . . . All the grandees and half the foreigners are there in their carriages, the *bourgeoisie* on foot staring at them and the beggars lining all the approaches. . . . The Pincio continues to beguile. It is a great resource.[19]

Besides the amiable crowd, the other great attraction of the Pincio was the "prospect," the panoramic vista it afforded of the city below.[20] Such a comprehensive view in a sense constituted the unitary or stationary equivalent of the earlier orientation drive, inasmuch as it visually consolidated many of the city's principal attractions.[21] Accordingly, from the very earliest days of their medium, it was a favorite subject for photographers.[22]

The Horblit collection contains views from the Monte Pincio by five photographers: Frédéric Flachéron, Giacomo Caneva, Robert Macpherson, James Anderson, and an anonymous member of the "Italian school." The pictures show a close family resemblance, with each including a bit of the garden, a fountain or part of the decorative parapet, and the city beyond. The most imposing single element in all the pictures is the dome of Saint Peter's.[23] To get a better perspective on the scene, we may consider a description by Nathaniel Hawthorne in *The Marble Faun*. Two of the characters, Hilda and Kenyon, while taking a stroll on the Pincio, stop at precisely the place where the aforementioned photographs were taken:

FIGURE 29. Giacomo Caneva. *Rome from Monte Pincio*, 1850s. Salted paper print; image: 19.5 x 26.7 cm., mount: 31.3 x 43.3 cm.

Still farther off appeared a mighty pile of buildings, surmounted by a vast dome, which all of us have shaped and swelled outward, like a huge bubble, to the utmost scope of our imaginations, long before we see it floating over the worship of the city. It may be most worthily seen from precisely the point where our two friends were now standing. At any nearer view the grandeur of St. Peter's hides itself behind the immensity of its separate parts, so that we see only the front, only the sides, only the pillared length and loftiness of the portico, and not the mighty whole. But at this distance the entire outline of the world's cathedral, as well as that of the palace of the world's chief priest, is taken in at once. In such remoteness, moreover, the imagination is not debarred from lending its assistance, even while we have the reality before our eyes, and helping the weakness of human sense to do justice to so grand an object.[24]

As Hawthorne perceived, one of the great advantages of the long view is that it permits the free play of fantasy. Distance, along with the miniaturization it imposes, conceals the various drawbacks and inconveniences of life in the real city. The visitor is literally and figuratively elevated above the congestion, the dirt, the traffic, and the noise, and the sylvan setting of the Pincio makes the contrast all the more pleasurable. In each of the photographs, the foreground is occupied by plants and fountains, or by the decorative balustrade that marks the edge of the hill. Despite the travel narratives' constant reminders of the crowds that throng the place, the photographs are for the most part remarkably empty of people; the one exception is Caneva's view, with its inclusion of a figure who is most likely the photographer himself. And even this man, thanks to his impressive beard and his bohemian outfit, can be assimilated into the category of the picturesque, like one of the *pifferari*, the city's itinerant pipers.[25] There is thus no unseemly intrusion by the modern world to detract from the viewer's enjoyment of the interplay between the idyllic garden and the now-diminutive cityscape.

The panorama from the Monte Pincio, as depicted in these photographs, is neither simple nor self-evident; it is, rather, carefully constructed. As Roland Barthes suggests in his allusive meditation on the Eiffel Tower, such an extensive view from above is at once complex and dialectical:

> On the one hand it is a euphoric vision, for it can slide slowly, lightly the entire length of a continuous image of [the city]; . . . but, on the other hand, this very continuity engages the mind in a certain struggle, it seeks to be deciphered, we must find *signs* within it, a familiarity proceeding from history and from myth.[26]

Barthes goes on to describe how viewers attempt to orient themselves by identifying the most significant landmarks. The successful performance of such a survey functions as a kind of initiation in that it allows the viewer to claim familiarity with the city. As Barthes asserts in the closing line of his essay, when one is looking at a city from a lofty vantage point, "one can feel oneself cut off from the world and yet the owner of a world."[27]

Precisely because of the attitudes superimposed on them by the foreign viewer, the photographic images of "Rome from the Pincio" cannot represent an uncomplicated celebration of the city. The park was prized simultaneously for its formal beauty and for its social informality, which presented ample opportunity for the flirtatious exchange of glances. In describing its promenade, the *passegiatta*, Henry James observed that "Europe is the continent of the practiced stare," and went on to praise the European woman's coquettish expertise in the "manner to play in public."[28] As James suggested, the English or American visitor expected to find such open flirtation in the south, where the warmth of the climate was thought to express itself in the morals of the "natives." They were seen as living closer to nature and thus being somehow both more indolent and more erotically

FIGURE 30.   Frédéric A. Flachéron. *Temple of Vesta and Fountain*, 1850s. Albumen silver print; image: 23.3 x 32.8 cm., mount: 27.9 x 39.5 cm.

active than the proper, repressed strangers from chillier lands.[29] In his famous novella, James used the Pincio as the setting for the scandalous public display of the liaison between his American heroine, Daisy Miller, and her Italian beau. The garden served at once as a refuge from the city and as a site for a bit of agreeably illicit visual pleasure.

Such visual pleasure was not, however, either necessarily illicit or limited to the park proper: the Pincio was valued as well for the view it afforded of the city below. There, the largest presence on the skyline—the most readily identifiable sign, in Barthes's terms—was of course Saint Peter's. George Hillard wrote:

> When Rome is viewed from a distance, the dome of St. Peter's is the central point of observation, and seems to be gathering the rest of the city under its enormous wings. It is so with thoughts and associations. St. Peter's is the first object of interest, around which all others group themselves.[30]

It is a commonplace among the travel narratives that the very sight of the dome ful-filled long-standing expectations,[31] a satisfaction that must surely have had as much to do with its singularity as with its scale: its sheer size cannot fully account for its prominence in the photographic views from the Pincio. Throughout the world, certain buildings have come to symbolize their city or even their culture as a whole. The Eiffel Tower, the Kremlin, and the Taj Mahal all have such an elusive quality of cultural resonance. What Barthes says of the Eiffel Tower is equally true of Saint Peter's: "As the major sign of a people and of a place . . . it belongs to the universal language of travel."[32] The recognition of its presence was a guarantee that the traveler was participating in the genuine experi-ence of Rome.

As with the Pincian *passegiatta*, the interest aroused by Saint Peter's was both aes-thetic and social. The great cathedral belonged to the sublime tradition of Italian art, pri-marily because Michelangelo had had a hand in its design. But more important, and more problematic, was its symbolic function, embodying the religious status of Rome as the in-stitutional center of Catholicism. In the passage quoted above, Hawthorne refers to the "world's cathedral" immediately after disparaging the dynasty of popes who have misled, or actively oppressed, the credulous. Such sentiments recur repeatedly in the writings of travelers from the mainly Protestant north. We have already noted Margaret Fuller's opin-ions, and writers otherwise so different as Charles Dickens and Mark Twain shared with her a strong antipathy toward the Catholic Church. Twain, for example, imagined the monologue of an Italian peasant describing a stay in America, whose first comment is, "I saw there a country which has no overshadowing Mother Church." Twain, in his own voice, then goes on to denounce the "monster Church of St. Peter."[33] In this light, the photographs from the Pincio may also be seen as evincing the dialectical tension between the ideal aesthetic appeal of the vista and the reality at least as it was perceived by visitors of the autocratic power of the pope and the enduring influence of Catholic superstition.[34]

Ironically, one of the other exemplary vantage points for a panoramic view was from the top of the dome of Saint Peter's itself. Mark Twain approached it with his customary dismissiveness ("Of course we ascended to the summit of the dome. . . . It was as close and hot as an oven") but in the end was forced to admit that the "panorama is varied, extensive, beautiful to the eye, and more illustrious in history than any other in Europe." The re-sponse of another American, J. T. Headley, was more typical, and especially noteworthy for its last sentence: "The mind became perfectly stupefied with the crowd of images and emotions that overwhelmed it. Glorious old Rome, that '*coup d'oeil*,' has become a part of my existence. It is daguerreotyped on my heart forever."[35]

FIGURE 31.   Tommaso Cuccioni. *Temple of Vesta*, 1850s. Albumen silver print; image: 22.9 x 31.6 cm., mount: 37.6 x 49.4 cm.

III

By far the most important ancient site on the traveler's itinerary in Rome was the Colosseum, followed by the Forum.[36] The city also offered many other monuments for the visitor interested in antiquity, with one of the most popular of these being the Temple of Vesta in the Forum Boarium (now known as the Piazza della Bocca della Verità), next to the Tiber.[37] Probably built in the time of Augustus, the circular shrine was subsequently converted into a Catholic church and eventually dedicated to Santa Maria del Sole; the fountain was added to the piazza in the early eighteenth century. From photography's earliest days, this site seems to have been a favorite subject for the medium's practitioners.[38] The Horblit collection contains photographs, either of the fountain and the temple or of the temple alone, by Flachéron, Caneva (attributed), Macpherson, and Cuccioni.[39]

The nineteenth-century guidebooks and travel narratives are unanimous in their praise of this attraction. Sophia Hawthorne, wife of Nathaniel, voiced a representative, if slightly extravagant, appreciation of the temple:

> It is of Parian marble, once pure white—a small circular cella surrounded by a colonnade of Corinthian fluted pillars. One column only has fallen. . . . I never saw anything built by human hands so simple and so lovely. Oh the divine sobriety of Grecian art! What a pattern for manners! It seems like a flower.[40]

Murray's guidebook is more subdued, but equally enthusiastic: "This elegant little temple has been for ages the admiration of travellers, and the numerous bronze models of it have made it better known than perhaps any other relic of Rome."[41] Given the fame of the Colosseum, the claim that this temple was the best-known monument of Roman antiquity can hardly be taken at face value. It is nonetheless worth asking, What made it so appealing that it was reproduced in innumerable miniatures and photographed with such uncommon frequency? The first answer is that the building was, and remains today, more or less intact. It still had nineteen of its original twenty columns; its only apparent flaw was that it had lost its ancient entablature and roof. Another factor that added to its attractiveness was that the piazza in which it stood was relatively secluded, tucked away from the distractions of the main squares and thoroughfares. Here the temple could be seen by itself, cleansed by time of the contamination of ordinary day-to-day concerns. Thanks to its preservation and its setting, it required no laborious imaginary reconstruction, as did the Roman Forum, but instead permitted the visitor to imagine that he or she was in the presence of authentic antiquity.

Because the outline of the structure was complete, its shape, like the dome of Saint Peter's, was immediately recognizable, thereby bestowing on even the neophyte visitor a sense of expertise. Thus Sophia Hawthorne could comment knowingly on the new roof, calling it "as ugly as possible," an assessment echoed by (or echoing) Octavian Blewitt's, in Murray's guidebook: "The entablature has entirely disappeared, and the roof has been replaced by an ugly covering of red tiles." Also joining the chorus was George Hillard, who noted that a "very ugly roof of red tiles is crushed down directly upon the capitals of the columns." The tone of such remarks makes it clear that participation in the near-universal condemnation of the roof—which is clearly visible in photographs of the site—demonstrated the writer's superior taste.[42]

Although there was another ancient shrine nearby—the so-called Temple of Fortuna Virilis (whose corner is just visible at the right of some of the photographs)[43]—the Temple of Vesta shared its own piazza only with the fountain mentioned above. For the foreign visitor, Hillard claimed, "the fountains in Rome are among its most delightful features: the stranger is never out of the sound of their dash and play."[44] This particular example was not nearly so famous or so elaborate as the Fontana di Trevi or the tripartite fountains in the Piazza Navona; nor was it in itself important enough to draw the travelers. Nonetheless, its age and classicizing statuary—the bowl was supported by entwined tritons—made it a thoroughly respectable companion to the temple: in purely visual terms, the fountain's twisting silhouette nicely complemented the austere lines of the ancient shrine. Photographs, in fact, often enhanced the effect of the juxtaposition because their compression of visual space set the two structures almost side by side within the frame.[45]

In addition to its decorative effect, the fountain also served a more practical purpose, as a watering trough for cattle and horses. The presence in the piazza of the animals and peasants was the final element confirming the picturesque foreignness of the scene. Flachéron's photograph in the Horblit collection, *Temple of Vesta and Fountain*, shows the fountain surrounded by bullock carts, with two men, possibly the drivers, reclining on the temple steps. Such images played on a number of themes both familiar and congenial to the tourist. The more erudite visitor could make a historical, or etymological, connection to what was thought to be the original function of the Forum Boarium; Sir George Head, for example, declared, "It is not to be wondered at that a place thus identified from the earliest ages with so many and various reminiscences relating to cattle was selected in the days of the Empire for the purpose of a cattle-market and called the Forum Boarium."[46]

But even more significantly, the continuing presence within the city of such rustic types reinforced the tourists' conviction that Rome had largely escaped the pressures of modernization, remaining a traditional agricultural community. Put another way, the north was the site of change, progress, and scientific and commercial advancement, while the south maintained a kind of Edenic sameness.[47]

Just as the long view from the Pincio assembled many of the major Roman sites into a single composition for the photographers and their audience, the near view of the Temple of Vesta and its neighboring fountain functioned as a compact sample of the attractions of Rome. In drawing such connections between the photographic images and contemporaneous travel accounts, I am not suggesting that the makers of the views were intentionally crafting religious and cultural allegories; but it is true that the photographers could count on a fairly predictable set of responses from their audience. The audience, in turn, could rely on the photographers to provide images that coincided with their own preconceptions, at once reflecting and reinforcing their vision of an ideal Rome.

FIGURE 32.   Robert Macpherson. *Temple of Vesta and the House of Rienzi*, between 1858 and 1868. Albumen silver print; image: 27.7 x 40.3 cm., mount: 47.5 x 63.3 cm.

ACKNOWLEDGMENTS

I would like to thank Anne Anninger and Julie Mellby of the Houghton Library for their patience during the long gestation of this paper, and for their generous assistance with all aspects of the project. I would also like to thank Elizabeth Bobrick for her careful reading and insightful suggestions. Needless to say, none of the aforementioned is responsible for any errors or omissions that remain.

Notes

1. For the name of the temple, see note 37 below.

2. For a historical survey of the phenomenon, see Christopher Hibbert, *The Grand Tour* (London: Thames and Methuen, 1987). In late 1996 the Tate Gallery mounted an exhibition of paintings, prints, drawings, and artifacts from the period and published a richly illustrated catalog: Andrew Wilton and Ilaria Bignamini, eds., *Grand Tour: The Lure of Italy in the Eighteenth Century* (London: The Tate Gallery, 1996).

3. See James Buzard, *The Beaten Track* (Oxford: Oxford University Press, 1993). I have not yet been able to consult Lynne Withey, *Grand Tours and Cooks' Tours: A History of Leisure Travel, 1750–1915* (New York: William Morrow, 1997).

4. See William Stowe, *Going Abroad* (Princeton: Princeton University Press, 1994).

5. This phrase serves as the subtitle of *Excursions Daguerriennes*, published in Paris by N. M. P. Lerebours between 1840 and 1843; see T. N. Gidal, "Lerebours' *Excursions Daguerriennes*," in Kathleen Collins, ed., *Shadow and Substance* (Albuquerque: University of New Mexico Press, 1990), 57–85. For the Italian views in this collection, see Italo Zannier, "*Excursions Daguerriennes* in Italia," *Fotologia* 10 (1988): 6–17.

6. Stowe provides an illuminating analysis of the relationship between travel and writing, arguing that writing represented a way to legitimize an activity that might otherwise be dismissed as frivolous or self-indulgent: *Going Abroad*, 3–15.

7. Margaret Fuller, *These Sad but Glorious Days: Dispatches from Europe, 1846–1850*, ed. L. Reynolds and S. B. Smith (New Haven: Yale University Press, 1991), 136.

8. She declares, for example, in a letter of January 1850, "Not only Jesuitism must go, but the Roman Catholic religion must go. The Pope cannot retain even his spiritual power. The influence of the clergy is too perverting, too foreign to every hope of advancement and health" (ibid., 321). See also William Vance, *America's Rome* (New Haven: Yale University Press, 1989), 2: 130–35.

9. There have been many studies of Fuller's life and work. See, most recently, Joan Von Mehren, *Minerva and the Muse: A Life of Margaret Fuller* (Amherst, Mass.: University of Massachusetts Press, 1994), and *Eve Kornfeld, Margaret Fuller: A Brief Biography with Documents* (Boston: Bedford Books, 1997).

10. Fuller, *These Sad but Glorious Days*, 168.

11. Karl Baedeker, *Handbook for Travelers: Central Italy* (Leipzig: Karl Baedeker, 1881), 118–20. For discussions of the role guidebooks played in the rise of mass travel, see Buzard, *The Beaten Track*, 64–77, and Stowe, *Going Abroad*, 29–54.

12. "Murray and Baedeker had invented an imperious and apparently ubiquitous authority small enough to fit in a tourist's pocket. They preceded the tourist, making the crooked straight and the rough places plain for the tourist's hesitant footsteps; they accompanied the tourist on the path they had beaten, directing gazes and prompting responses" (Buzard, *The Beaten Track*, 75).

13. Another group the tourist could expect to encounter was beggars. The standard guidebooks were unanimous in strictly advising the visitor against any almsgiving. In the words of Baedeker, "[Begging] continues to be one of those national nuisances to which the traveller must habituate himself. . . . The average Italian beggar is a mere speculator, and not a deserving object of charity" (*Handbook for Travelers*, xvii). Such remarks are worth noting because, like Fuller's comments about Catholicism, they epitomize some of the prevalent attitudes on the part of foreign visitors toward Italians.

14. Octavian Blewitt, Murray's *Hand-Book for Travellers in Central Italy and Rome* (London: John Murray, 1850), 293.

15. John Murray, *A Handbook for Travellers in Central Italy*, part 2: *Rome and Its Environs*, 4th ed. (London: John Murray, 1856), xv; after the quoted sentences, Murray supplies the addresses where Macpherson's photographs could be bought. A quarter of a century later, the 1881 Baedeker guide lists ten commercial outlets for photographic views and has separate headings for "Photographs for Artistic Purposes (Reproductions of Sketches, Pictures, Etc.)" and "Portraits"; it even cites one vendor of "Cheap Photographs" (Baedeker, *Handbook*, 110).

16. There exist several studies devoted to photography in nineteenth-century Italy. A succinct historical survey of the period may be found in the introductory essays in Dyveke Helsted et al., *Rome in Early Photographs 1846–1878*, trans. Ann Thornton (Copenhagen: Thorvaldsen Museum, 1977), and a biographical catalog of photographers is included in Piero Becchetti, *Fotografi e fotografia in Italia* (Rome: Edizioni Quasar, 1978). See also the comprehensive bibliography in *History of Photography*, Maria Antonella Pelizzari, ed., 20, no. 1 (1996): 73–77.

17. "One is immediately struck by the frequency with which photographers like Macpherson borrowed and recycled pictorial conventions established by printmakers very much earlier": Ray McKenzie, "The Cradle and Grave of Empires: Robert Macpherson and the Photography of Nineteenth-Century Rome," *The Photographic Collector* 4, no. 2 (1983): 221–34, the quoted sentence on 224. See also A. Szegedy-Maszak, "A Perfect Ruin: Nineteenth-Century Views of the Colosseum," *Arion*, 3d ser., 2, no. 1 (1992): 115–41; and "Forum Romanum/Campo Vaccino," *History of Photography* 20, no. 1 (1996): 24–32.

18. Baedeker, *Handbook*, 119.

19. Henry James, "From a Roman Note-Book," in *Collected Travel Writings: The Continent*, ed. Richard Howard (New York: Library of America, 1993), 475–77. Nathaniel Hawthorne, characteristically, is more sardonic: "The Pincian Hill is the favorite promenade of the Roman aristocracy. At the present day, however, like most other Roman possessions, it belongs less to the native inhabitants than to the barbarians from Gaul, Britain, and beyond the sea, who have established a peaceful usurpation over whatever is enjoyable or memorable in the Eternal City" (*The Marble Faun*, ch. 12). The American painter Maurice Prendergast, visiting the city in the late 1890s, painted the colorful stream of carriages, strollers, and loungers: see Theodore Stebbins, Jr., *The Lure of Italy: American Artists and the Italian Experience* (Boston and New York: Museum of Fine Arts, Boston, and Harry N. Abrams, 1992), 252–54, and Vance, *America's Rome* 2: 265–67.

20. The observation by the American travel writer George Stillman Hillard is typical: "It is only necessary to choose a commanding position in Rome, to find pictures unique in themselves, attractive to the eye and delightful to recall. The view from the Pincian Hill is that with which strangers are most familiar," *Six Months in Italy*, 3d. ed. (Boston: Ticknor & Co., 1864), 2: 18–19.

21. "The charm of this promenade [on the Pincio] is the splendid prospects it commands on every side. . . . On the west, where a fine terrace is formed by a wall enclosing three sides of a square, the view comprises the greater part of the modern city; including the Janiculum, the Vatican, St. Peter's, and the regular outline of the Monte Mario, crowned with its dark line of cypresses" (ibid., 2: 41). I have called such panoramas "Best General Views" by analogy with the popular nineteenth-century "Best General View" of Yosemite (Szegedy-Maszak, "Forum Romanum/Campo Vaccino," 27 and note 24).

22. The earliest example of which I am aware is a daguerreotype from June 1841 by A. J. Ellis; now in the Science Museum in London, it is reproduced in Piero Becchetti and Carlo Pietrangeli, *Roma in dagherrotipia* (Rome: Edizioni Quasar, 1979), 123, and in Wendy Watson, *Images of Italy: Photography in the Nineteenth Century* (South Hadley, Mass.: Mount Holyoke College Art Museum, 1980), 28.

23. In 1865 the American artist Sanford Robinson Gifford painted *St. Peter's from the Pincian Hill* from a vantage almost the same as Macpherson's (reproduced in Watson, *Images of Italy*, 39); see Stebbins, *The Lure of Italy*, 230–31.

24. Hawthorne, *The Marble Faun*, ch. 12.

25. The same man appears in two more photographs by Caneva in the Horblit collection: seated at the foot of the tall cross in the middle of the Colosseum (*Interior of the Coliseum, Looking East*), and next to the Arch of Titus (*Arch of Titus with Figure*). I have not yet been able either to confirm the identification or to consult Piero Becchetti, *Giacomo Caneva e la scuola fotografica romana 1847–1855* (Florence: Alinari, 1989). For the picturesque population of Rome, see below and note 47.

26. Roland Barthes, *The Eiffel Tower and Other Mythologies*, trans. Richard Howard (New York: Hill and Wang, 1979), 10. Although not taken from above, the other conventional Best General View of Rome follows the same general scheme: a panorama from near the Porta Ripetta on the Tiber, it includes the river, Saint Peter's, and the Castel Sant'Angelo. There are dozens, if

not hundreds, of variations on this latter view. The Horblit collection contains examples by Anderson (*View of Rome with St. Peter's in the Background*), Constant (*View of the Tiber and Castel Sant'Angelo*), and Macpherson (*The Castle and Bridge of St. Angelo with the Vatican*). For reproductions of similar studies from Excursions Daguerriennes, see Zannier, "*Excursions Daguerriennes in Italia*," 13; by Caneva, see Watson, *Images of Italy*, 22; by Altobelli, see Helsted et al., *Rome in Early Photographs*, 148.

27. Barthes, *The Eiffel Tower*, 17.

28. James, "From a Roman Note-Book," 476; see also Elizabeth Block, "The Rome of Henry James," in Annabel Patterson, ed., *Roman Images* (Baltimore: Johns Hopkins University Press, 1984), 141–62.

29. See John Pemble, *The Mediterranean Passion: Victorians and Edwardians in the South* (Oxford: Oxford University Press, 1988), 96–109, 149–64.

30. Hillard, *Six Months in Italy* 1: 205.

31. As Hillard notes, Saint Peter's was typically the traveler's first destination. For example, the American J. T. Headley wrote, "After I had become domiciled, the first object I sought was St. Peter's" in *Letters from Italy*, rev. ed. (New York: Charles Scribner, 1851), 113; and Charles Dickens, "Immediately on going out the next day [after our arrival], we hurried off to St. Peter's" in *Pictures from Italy* (1846, reprint, New York: The Ecco Press, 1988), 107. Other such comments by other visitors could be multiplied indefinitely.

32. Barthes, *The Eiffel Tower*, 4.

33. *The Innocents Abroad*, ed. Guy Cardwell (New York: Library of America, 1984), ch. 26; the two quotations, on 210 and 213. For the significance of this passage, see Vance, *America's Rome* 2: 204–06. Dickens anticipates objections from his Catholic readers—"When I mention any exhibition that impressed me as absurd or disagreeable, I do not seek to connect it . . . with any essentials of their creed" (*Pictures from Italy*, 2)—and then goes on to say of Saint Peter's, "It is not religiously impressive or affecting. It is an immense edifice, . . . and it tires itself with wandering round and round" (ibid., 109).

34. For a comprehensive analysis of American attitudes, see Vance, *America's Rome*, vol. 2: *Catholic and Contemporary Rome*.

35. Twain, *The Innocents Abroad*, 215, 216; Headley, *Letters from Italy*, 163.

36. See Szegedy-Maszak, "A Perfect Ruin" and "Forum Romanum/Campo Vaccino."

37. "No less than ten names have been attributed to this graceful round temple," observed the nineteenth-century archaeologist Rodolfo Lanciani in *The Ruins and Excavations of Ancient Rome* (Boston and New York: Houghton Mifflin Co., 1897), 515. Lanciani himself opted for the "Temple of Mater Matuta," but the identification is so uncertain that the building is now simply called the "round temple": see Ernest Nash, *Pictorial Dictionary of Ancient Rome* (New York: Praeger, 1961), 1: 411–13, and Lawrence Richardson, Jr., *A New Topographical Dictionary of Ancient Rome* (Baltimore: Johns Hopkins University Press, 1992), s.v. "Forum Boarium," 162–64. In the following pages I will refer to it as the Temple of Vesta to maintain consistency with the nineteenth-century sources.

38. Helsted et al., *Rome in Early Photographs*, no. 126. A study of the temple and fountain is included in *Excursions Daguerriennes;* see Zannier, "Excursions Daguerriennes in Italia," cover (in negative); and Becchetti and Pietrangeli, *Roma in dagherrotipia*, 38.

39. The Horblit collection also includes versions by Macpherson (*View of the Cloaca Maxima Temple of Vesta, Church of the "Bocca della Verita*, etc."), and Cuccioni (*Temple of Vesta, Church of Santa Maria in Cosmedin*) of a view from across the Tiber, depicting the cluster of buildings around the piazza as well as the arched top of the Cloaca Maxima in the embankment below. For another, similar study by Eugène Constant, see Watson, *Images of Italy*, 23.

40. Sophia Hawthorne, *Notes in England and Italy* (New York: G. P. Putnam's Sons, 1878), 200.

41. Blewitt, *Murray's Hand-Book for Travellers*, 337. George Hillard permits himself some humor on the same topic: "It is a pretty toy of a building; too small, to borrow an expression of Horace Walpole's, to live in, and too large to hang at one's watch-chain. Its form and features are multiplied in an immense progeny of bronze models and inkstands, to which it has given birth" (*Six Months in Italy* 1: 324).

42. S. Hawthorne, *Notes in England and Italy*, 200; Blewitt, Murray's *Hand-Book for Travellers*, 337; Hillard, *Six Months in Italy* 1: 324. One dissenter is the British ex-

patriate and aesthete A. J. C. Hare: "The modern overhanging roof of the temple has been much objected to, as it replaces an entablature like that on the temple of the Sibyl at Tivoli; but artists admire the exquisite play of light and shade caused by its rugged tiles, and, finding it a perfect 'subject,' wish for no change" in *Walks in Rome*, 8th ed. (New York: George Routledge & Sons, 1882), 154.

43. One of the earliest such studies is a calotype made by Calvert Jones in 1846; it is reproduced in Helsted, *Rome in Early Photographs*, 124; see also Hans P. Kraus, Jr., *Sun Pictures V: The Reverend Calvert R. Jones*, text by Larry J. Schaaf (New York: Hans P. Kraus, Jr., 1990), 46. Two of the pictures in the Horblit collection—by Flachéron (*Temple of Vesta, Rome*) and Macpherson (*Temple of Vesta and the Fountain, Taken in Summer*)—are taken from almost exactly the same point of view.

44. Hillard, *Six Months in Italy* 1, 410; on the previous page, Hillard declares, "There are one hundred and eight public fountains in Rome. The private ones are much more numerous. . . . No city in Christendom is so bountifully furnished in this respect as Rome." The presence of the fountain in the views of the Pincio by Macpherson and Anderson (*View of the Cathedral of St. Peter and the Vatican Taken from Behind the Fountain of Monte Pincio*) may also be noted here.

45. I owe this observation to Carlo Pietrangeli. Commenting on Macpherson's picture *Temple of Vesta and the Fountain, Taken in Summer*, Pietrangeli says, "Il fenomeno di schiacciamento della prospettiva che si nota talvolta nelle vecchie fotografie, è particolarmente accentuato in questa veduta" in Piero Becchetti and Carlo Pietrangeli, *Un inglese fotografo a Roma, Robert Macpherson* (Rome: Edizioni Quasar, 1987), 97.

46. *Rome: A Tour of Many Days* (London: Longman, Brown, Green and Longmans, 1849), 2: 125. This explanation for the name has been rejected by most modern scholars: "There is no evidence that [the Forum Boarium] was ever the cattle market of Rome. . . .[Some Roman sources derived the name,] probably correctly, from the Aeginetan bronze statue of an ox, believed to mark the beginning of the pomerium of Romulus there" (Richardson, *A New Topographical Dictionary of Ancient Rome*, 162–63).

47. I have written elsewhere about the fact that in the eyes of many foreign visitors, the Roman population consisted almost exclusively of priests, peasants, and beggars; see Szegedy-Maszak, "A Perfect Ruin," especially 127 and note 36, and "Forum Romanum/Campo Vaccino," especially 24–25 and notes 9–11. Modern anthropologists have pointed out that until very recently, even scholarly accounts of other cultures have generally characterized them as timeless, harmonious, internally homogeneous, and unchanging. See, for example, Renato Rosaldo, *Culture and Truth* (rev. ed.; Boston: Beacon Press, 1993).

The fondness for a bit of local color in the photographs in some cases led to imaginative alterations of the original image. In the view of the Temple of Vesta included in *Excursions Daguerriennes*, for instance, the engraver who transcribed the daguerreotype inserted a group of peasants playing bocce in the piazza. Even Robert Macpherson, widely praised for the lucid objectivity of his architectural studies, seems, in his picture *Temple of Vesta and House of Rienzi*, to have painted in one of the figures seated on the steps of the building.

"Gymnastics of the Soul"
The Clinical Aesthetics of
Duchenne de Boulogne

Robert Sobieszek

To render our most secret emotions and passions with as much delicacy as vigor, it is necessary to know what organs nature employs to express them.[1]

I first chanced upon the photography of Duchenne de Boulogne in the summer of 1966, while paging through Charles Darwin's *The Expression of the Emotions in Man and Animals* in the library of the George Eastman House. The images of an old man grimacing in terror and agony seemed like the forgotten record of some sort of arcane, malevolent experiment (figure 33). These bizarre portrayals of the tortured geometries of the human countenance continued to haunt me for years; I was reminded of one in particular, an oval collotype showing the old man being shocked by electrodes into a rictus of abject horror, whenever I encountered any film version of *Frankenstein; or, The Modern Prometheus* (1818), Mary Shelley's classic novel of galvanic reanimation. Duchenne's work also kindled my interest in just how artists and scientists have used photography to try to decipher our emotions, our psyches, and our hiddenmost pathologies. Intermittent research into this question eventually led to a general lecture that I delivered at the invitation of Light Gallery in New York in the spring of 1972. Shortly thereafter, I met Harrison Horblit, who had joined the board of trustees of the Eastman House, and I soon became friends with him and his wife, Jean. My frequent visits to their Connecticut home and our many pleasant conversations were made even more memorable by Harrison's giving me the opportunity to examine his exceptional collection of early scientific literature and nineteenth-century photography. It was here, in this collection, among first editions of Kepler, Newton, Diderot and D'Alembert, and William Henry Fox Talbot, that I finally held an actual copy of Duchenne's *Mécanisme de la physionomie humaine*, with its unforgettable photographs.[2] I am therefore especially pleased and honored to be able to contribute in some small way to this celebration of a remarkable collector and an unparalleled collection.

Guillaume-Benjamin Duchenne (he later added the name Armand) was born in Boulogne-sur-Mer in 1806. He received a bachelor's degree in letters in Douai, studied

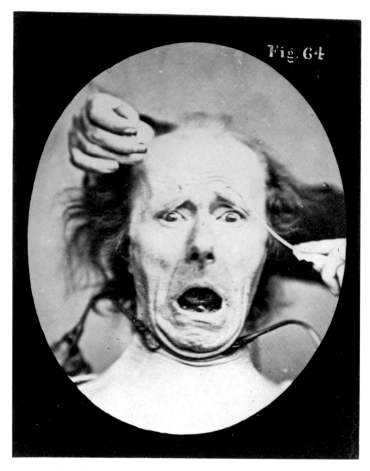

FIGURE 33.   Guillaume-Benjamin Duchenne. *The Muscle of Fright, of Terror* from *Mécanisme de la Physionomie Humaine* (Paris, Veuve Jules Renouard, 1862), fig. 64. Albumen silver print; image: 11.9 x 9.2 cm., volume: 28.6 x 19.2 cm.

medicine and applied electricity at the Académie de Médecine in Paris, and opened a practice in his native Boulogne, where in 1835 he began experimenting with therapeutic "electropuncture."[3] Returning to Paris in 1842—he would reside there until his death, in 1875—he continued his experiments and developed what he called *électrisation localisée*, a technique that used faradic shock to excite the contraction of specific muscles.[4] He was a pioneer in the fields of kinesiology and neurology, and his work led to the diagnosis and treatment of such physiological disorders as muscular dystrophy and atrophic paralysis.

While the 1862 treatise *Mécanisme de la physionomie humaine*, in which he applied "localized electrization" to the "electrophysiological and aesthetic study of facial expression,"[5] is neither the best-known nor perhaps the most important of Duchenne's many works, it nonetheless has a place at the center of a number of discourses, not the least of these being the consideration of the nature of the human psyche, how it expresses itself, and how it is represented. But even that would be of little moment here if this little-discussed publication were not artistically and photographically both singular and compelling.

THE MECHANISM OF HUMAN PHYSIOGNOMY

In an amazing confluence of medical science, psychology, the fine arts, and theater, Duchenne de Boulogne's *Mécanisme de la physionomie humaine, ou Analyse électro-physiologique de l'expression des passions applicable à la pratique des arts plastiques* sought conclusively and scientifically to chart the "grammar and orthography of human facial expression" in a three-part text and an "atlas" of photographic plates.[6] Like physiognomists and phrenologists before him, Duchenne trusted that the human face was a map whose features could be codified into universal taxonomies of inner states; unlike them, he was skeptical of the face's ability to express moral character. Like the anatomists and physiologists who preceded him, Duchenne based his myological experiments on precise scientific methods and a thorough knowledge of existing literature; he broke rank with them, however, by being the very first to substitute experimentation for pure observation.[7] Finally, like a number of earlier theorists, Duchenne emphasized the application of his findings to the study of the fine arts; but he differed from his predecessors in being "convinced of the impossibility of popularizing or even of publishing this research without the aid of photography."[8] He therefore taught himself this art in order to be able to document his experiments.

At first glance, Duchenne's *Mécanisme de la physionomie humaine* looks like little more than a minor and idiosyncratic oddity.[9] To judge by its title and the author's stated intentions, it would seem to be an essay on human physiognomy, or a study of the expression of human emotions, simply another in a long line of similar texts that had been appearing with some regularity since the Renaissance. After outlining the background of the study and the principles according to which it was conducted in a lengthy preliminary section ("General Considerations"), Duchenne proceeds to define the fundamental expressive gestures of the human face and to link each of these gestures with a specific facial muscle or muscle group. He identifies thirteen primary emotions whose expression is either enabled by a single muscle or seen in conjunction with the expression of another: "attention," "reflection," "aggression," "pain," "joy and benevolence," "lasciviousness," "sadness," "weeping and whimpering," "surprise," "fright," and "terror." In addition, he isolates the precise movements of each expression and separates these contractions into two distinct divisions, partial and combined. "Partial" contractions are caused by the movement of a single muscle or muscle group and include 1) those that are completely expressive on their own, 2) others that in themselves are incompletely expressive, 3) still others that are complementarily expressive through synergetic movement with another muscle or single group of muscles, and 4) those that are completely inexpressive. "Combined" contractions result from the excitation of a number of differing muscles at the same time to produce expressions that are either 1) expressive of complex emotions, 2) simply inexpressive grimaces, or 3) discordantly expressive, as when the muscle indicating joy is triggered along with that demonstrative of pain.

From an art-historical point of view, the *Mécanisme de la physionomie humaine* is notable for being the first publication on the expression of human emotions illustrated with actual photographs: startling and almost surreal images of men, women, and children whose facial features are so artificially distorted by what Duchenne called the "gymnastics of the soul"[10] that they frequently appear to present nothing more than wildly grotesque or utterly inchoate grimaces. Yet behind these evidently insane countenances, there lay a method. In most cases Duchenne had applied faradic shock to one muscle on the right side of the subject's face and to another, completely different muscle on the left; viewers were instructed to examine each half of the face in these photographs independently. For instance, plate 48 is captioned as follows: "On the left, electrical stimulation of *m. zygomaticus minor: mild weeping; pity*. On the right, moderate electrical stimulation of *m. zygomaticus major: feeble false laughter*"(figure 34).[11] In the book's "Scientific Section," Duchenne used as many as six living models, all but one of them patients of his, but his primary model in these photographs was the "old toothless man, with a thin face, whose features, without being absolutely ugly, approached ordinary triviality."[12]

Lest the reader conclude that a degree of torture or at least some sort of inhumane treatment was inherent in these experiments, the doctor from Boulogne was quick to point out,

> This subject [i.e., the old man] had reduced sensation. He was suffering from a complicated anaesthetic condition of the face. I was able to experiment on his face without causing him pain, to the extent that I could stimulate his individual muscles with as much precision and accuracy as if I were working with a still irritable cadaver.[13]

Duchenne took pains to assert that great care was required in limiting the amount of "electrical excitation" administered to each of his subjects, as too much of a shock would produce only a "grimace" instead of a real expression. He also insisted that in spite of being artificially induced, the expressions in his portraits remained "grippingly true."[14]

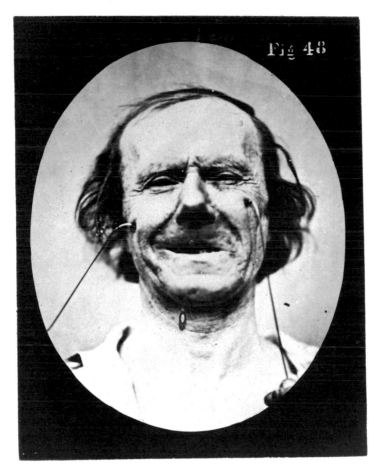

FIGURE 34. Guillaume-Benjamin Duchenne. *The Muscles of Weeping and Whimpering* from *Mécanisme de la Physionomie Humaine* (Paris, Veuve Jules Renouard, 1862), fig. 48. Albumen silver print; image: 12 x 9.2 cm., volume: 28.6 x 19.2 cm.

Having thus demonstrated in the "Scientific Section" the principal facts of the grammar and orthography of human facial expression "with the most complete empiricism," Duchenne in the "Aesthetic Section" defended his work against its critics and elaborated on his claim of having assembled a pictorial thesaurus of aesthetic beauty. Thus, in reply to criticism of his use of the ugly old man, Duchenne argued that his model was preferable to Adonis for "scientifically" outlining the lines of the face, asserting that by his very example he showed that any face could become spiritually beautiful, and that the alternative—animating the face of a corpse, which he had in fact already done—would have presented a far "more hideous and revolting spectacle."[15] In order to "placate those who possess 'a sense of beauty,'" a different series of electrophysiological studies were made and photographed to illustrate the set of "conditions that constitute beauty from the aesthetic point of view."[16] Whereas the "Scientific Section" was intended solely to exhibit the expressive lines of the face and the "truth of expression," here the "gesture and the pose together contribute to the expression; the trunk and the limbs must be photographed with as much care as the face so as to form an harmonious whole."[17] For these plates, Duchenne used a partially blind young woman who, in his mindlessly sexist opinion, "had become accustomed to the unpleasant sensation of this treatment" and was uncomprehending enough that he was "obliged to position her and dress her as if she were a mannequin" (figure 35).[18] This female model was also faradically stimulated in such a manner as to

FIGURE 35.   Guillaume-Benjamin Duchenne. *The Muscles of Joy and Benevolence* from *Mécanisme de la Physionomie Humaine* (Paris, Veuve Jules Renouard, 1862), fig. 35. Albumen silver print; image: 11.6 x 8.9 cm., volume: 28.6 x 19.2 cm.

ROBERT SOBIESZEK

enact a different expression on either side of her face; Duchenne advised that looking at both sides simultaneously would reveal a "mere grimace," and again he urged the reader to examine each side carefully and separately.

In this "Aesthetic Section," Duchenne directed a set of complex and often irrational scenes of melodramatic histrionics by contrasting different facial expressions at the same time and in the same model, posed for this purpose in various fictional tableaux (figure 36). These eleven scenes for the "Aesthetic Section," which Duchenne admitted to having photographed himself with the aid of a laboratory assistant, form a curious collection of narrative "genre" scenes not entirely unlike other genre images produced by amateur and artist photographers of the time, though Duchenne's are infinitely more unorthodox in

FIGURE 36.   Guillaume-Benjamin Duchenne. *Aesthetic Electrophysiological Studies on the Mechanism of Human Facial Expression* from *Mécanisme de la Physionomie Humaine* (Paris, Veuve Jules Renouard, 1862), fig. 78. Albumen silver print; image. 11.6 x 9.2 cm., volume: 28.6 x 19.2 cm.

what they suggest. It was here, with these eleven photographic plates and their accompanying texts, that Duchenne's *Mécanisme de la physionomie humaine* broke decisively with traditional studies of physiognomy and the expressions of emotions, to become a strangely provocative addition to the literature of modern life and art in the nineteenth century.

A PHYSIOGNOMIC CULTURE

Explaining what lay beneath the dross and vagaries of human expressions was Duchenne's principal aim and had been one of the aims of Western science since Aristotle purportedly advised Alexander to select his counselors by their appearances.[19] Physiognomy—the term being derived from the Greek *phusis* ("nature") and *gnomon* ("interpretation")—refers to the precise science (or, if one must, the imprecise pseudoscience) of interpreting the neutral, static face in order to discern the hidden character and emotional qualities of the subject. Both ancient and modern physiognomists believed that the face was some sort of secret narrative to be read, deciphered, and decoded, with the true personality or character of the individual standing ready to be revealed by such a reading. The rote facial expressions found in classic theater, as well as those in history painting from Nicholas Poussin to Jacques Louis David and beyond, relate directly to a series of rules formulated by Cureau de la Chambre and René Descartes, which were then visually schematized and adroitly delineated by Charles Le Brun, First Painter to Louis XIV. Le Brun's opposing pairs of admiration/contempt, love/hatred, and joy/sadness were in turn analogous to the Racinian "elocution" of the soul that "oscillates" between poles of strictly articulated emotive states.[20] Physiognomics moreover sought to isolate what Leonardo da Vinci had called the "relevant traits" of the human face, and to create a system of immutable equations between certain features and specific moral characteristics, for example, between full lips and sensuality.[21] The most important monument and most influential theory of physiognomy was, of course, Johann Kaspar Lavater's four-volume *Physiognomische Fragmente zur Beförderung der Menschenkenntniss und Menschenliebe*, an unwieldy compilation of spurious observations, moralizing anecdotes, arcane mathematics, and importuning lectures published in Leipzig and Winterthur in 1775–78. Despite the work's flaws, the ardor with which Lavater (1741–1801) proselytized his ideas brought the *Fragmente* almost instant success as well as sharp criticism, setting the stage for what would amount to a nearly century-long "physiognomic culture" in Europe and America, and establishing a "physiognomic climate" in the context of which Duchenne would play out his experiments.[22]

Lavater, a Swiss theologian, firmly believed that the human face was foremost a clear and certain indicator of an individual's moral character. Facial beauty equaled virtue, and its opposite, ugliness, equaled vice; analysis of the forehead, eyes, eyebrows, nose, chin, and profile provided the key by which to discern intelligence and character. For Lavater, the study of the expression of the emotions was merely a banal, if necessary, sideline to physiognomic studies.[23] Passions and emotions were fleeting and immaterial; certitude of absolute moral character was what mattered, and that could be achieved only by studying the static and fixed countenance. His critics, for their part, were adamant that the static face revealed little, if anything, about a person; its expressive movements alone furnished a visual, albeit untrustworthy, access to its owner's inner state.

PATHOGNOMY AND MEDICAL SCIENCE

The physiognomic climate of the late eighteenth and entire nineteenth centuries fostered the development of a significant branch discipline of physiognomics, one that was much more "scientific" and increasingly concerned with facial myology and neurophysiology.[24] Duchenne de Boulogne explicitly aligned himself with this growing scientific and medical enterprise, which differed greatly from ancient zoological or astrological physiognomics, as well as from classical, Lavaterian physiognomics of moral character and the ideal.

This new branch's greatest break from Lavaterian physiognomics consisted in its recognition that the inert form of the head was for all practical purposes devoid of either independent meaning or access to any true inner state. According to the Scottish anatomist Sir Charles Bell (1774–1842), "Expression is even of more consequence than shape: it will light up features otherwise heavy; it will make us forget all but the quality of the mind."[25] In his turn, Duchenne argued that the "study of facial expression in movement, entirely omitted by Lavater, should precede the study of physiognomy at rest," adding that Lavater

> certainly would not have neglected as much as he did of the study of facial expression in movement, which should serve as the basis for the examination of the physiognomy at rest, had he been either an anatomist or a physiologist or a doctor or even a naturalist.[26]

Duchenne's words are revealing. In but one, critical respect, the nineteenth-century study of physiognomy in motion, or pathognomy (from the Greek *pathos*, meaning "suffering," "pain," or "disease"), followed the general development of what Michel Foucault called the "anatomo-pathological perception" in clinical medicine. This allowed the voices of anatomists such as Bell, physiologists such as Duchenne, pathologists such as Jean-Martin Charcot of the Salpêtrière asylum in Paris (about whom more later), and naturalists such as Darwin (1809–1882) to drown out the traditional chorus of philosophers such as

Descartes and moralists such as Lavater. The importance of these new voices, to quote Foucault, "does not prove that they were philosophers as well as doctors, but [rather] that, in this culture, medical thought is fully engaged in the philosophical status of man."[27]

Although Duchenne drew heavily on Bell's work on facial muscles and seconded his insistence on the need for artists fully to grasp the lessons taught by anatomical observation, he did not share the Scottish anatomist's interest in the motive expressions of exaggerated or extreme passions, as found in madness and insanity. In fact, he kept himself strangely apart from one of the last century's most intense medical and scientific discourses, on the "anatomo-pathological perception" of the insane—a discourse that occupied so many "alienists" and physiognomists in France alone, from Jean-Etienne-Dominique Esquirol and Etienne-Jean Georget at the start of the century to Henri Dagonet and Jean-Martin Charcot toward its close. Even Darwin considered the expressions of the insane at some length in *The Expression of the Emotions*.[28]

BEAUTY AND TRUTH

Duchenne may have avoided photographing the passions of the insane because of photography's technical limitations at the time; or perhaps he agreed with Darwin's conclusion that such photographs, whether staged or not, were essentially too subjective to be of much scientific value.[29] It seems far more likely, however, that the expressions of the emotions in the insane were ignored by Duchenne for aesthetic reasons, as such emotional expressions were simply not beautiful. Early in the "Scientific Section," Duchenne announces that he has sought to capture the "conditions that aesthetically constitute beauty,"[30] and he reiterates in the "Aesthetic Section" that it is his desire to portray the "conditions of beauty: beauty of form associated with exactness of the facial expression, pose, and gesture."[31] He chose the old man as his primary model, he explains, not to show nature's imperfections, but rather to "prove that, despite defects of shape and lack of plastic beauty, every human face can become morally beautiful through the accurate rendering of the soul's emotions."[32]

If the "accurate rendering" of emotions was a requisite for "moral beauty," the exact imitation of nature was for Duchenne the sine qua non of the finest art of whatever age. He asserted that despite making anatomical errors, the ancient Greek sculptors had unquestionably attained an ideal of beauty, but only because the nature they imitated was a "beautiful" one. "In other words," he believed, "they produced an *idealized naturalism*—two words whose combination may shock initially: but which perfectly convey my thought." In his own defense, Duchenne even went so far as to "correct" three widely revered classical sculptures, as well as the late-baroque essayist and poet Boileau's famous adage "Nothing but the truth is beautiful; truth alone is to be admired," proposing, in its stead, "Nothing is beautiful without truth."[33]

The "truth" of his pathognomic experiments could, Duchenne felt, be rendered only by photography. The muscular contractions of his subjects' expressions were too fleeting to be drawn or painted; "only photography, as truthful as a mirror, could attain such desirable perfection."[34] However, he warned in the "Scientific Section," "you can only transmit well what you perceive well. . . . Art does not rely only on technical skills. For my research, it was necessary to know how to put each expressive line into relief by a skillful play of light."[35] While admitting that the less-than-perfect German lenses used in the 1850s produced some distortion and lack of sharpness, Duchenne nonetheless insisted that these imperfections did not dilute the "truth and clarity" of the photographs, and that the "distribution of light is quite in harmony with the emotions that the expressive lines represent."[36]

If Duchenne stressed exactitude in rendering emotional expressions in art, in no way did or could he countenance the sacrifice of beauty. He favored such baroque artists as Rembrandt, Ribera, Guido Reni, and Salvator Rosa, and condemned modern realism as a style of art that "only shows us nature with her imperfections and even deformities, and that seems to prefer the ugly, the vulgar, or the trivial."[37]

Some of Duchenne's contemporaries, less dogmatic, argued for a more organic approach, a reconciliation of the two extremes of realism and idealism. In October 1866, the art critic Ernest Chesneau reviewed three contemporary publications on physiognomy, devoting most of his article to Duchenne's *Mécanisme*. Classical antiquity's achievement in perfecting an "ideal of material and plastic beauty" remained unparalleled, according to Chesneau, but modern art had exceeded antiquity in one respect:

> More ambitious, stronger, broader in its visions, and especially more elevated, modern art has succeeded in combining plastic beauty and, even more so, picturesque beauty with an emotional power mostly ignored by the ancients, a new element of action upon the soul, the heart, and the spirit. This aesthetic ability, almost unknown before our time and most often systematically neglected and scorned, is expression, by which I mean the moral expression of sentiments, sensations, intellectual faculties, and human passions visually translated by the mobile play of the physiognomy.[38]

Chesneau admired Duchenne's book absolutely and considered it an essential tool for furnishing contemporary artists with scientifically proven laws, not unlike those of perspective, by which the soul's expressions were governed.

In his 1867 essay "Sur la physionomie," the critic Louis-Emile-Edmond Duranty (1833–1880) asserted that traditional theories of expression were the result of overabstraction and insufficient observation of individuals in their actual settings, adding that "at the present moment, we are cleverer than Lavater, and he could not compete with a contemporary novelist."[39] "The best counsel to give those who want to recognize a man or men," Duranty concluded, "is to have much wit and wisdom in unraveling the entanglements because speech is a liar, action is hypocritical, and the physiognomy is delusive."[40] He was not alone in dismissing the conventional "lessons" of physiognomy and insisting on direct observation of individuals in their own context. Emile Zola's novels had begun to present

FIGURE 37.   Guillaume-Benjamin Duchenne. *Further Aesthetic Electrophysiological Studies* from *Mécanisme de la Physionomie Humaine* (Paris, Veuve Jules Renouard, 1862), fig. 79. Albumen silver print; image: 11.4 x 9.1 cm., volume: 28.6 x 19.2 cm.

far more complicated and penetrating psychological characterizations than those found in the works of, say, Honoré de Balzac, who himself had depended greatly on Lavater.[41] For his part, Edgar Degas (who used Duranty as his model for a genre scene begun in 1870, alternately entitled *Sulking* or *The Banker*) had written to himself, in a notebook he kept in 1868–72, "Make of the *tête d'expression* (in academic parlance) a study of modern feelings. It is Lavater, but a Lavater more relative, as it were, with accessory symbols at times."[42]

Degas's "more relative" is a key here. Duchenne was convinced that he had inductively discovered the immutable laws of human facial expression; regardless of any infinite variety of facial features or any simultaneous expression of conflicting emotions, he steadfastly held to a positivist view of what expression signified. For him, the inner workings of the self determined the expression worn on the face, whether volitional or not. More progressive writers such as Duranty and artists such as Degas could not remain so assured; for them, personality was immanent in physically mutable and often artificial appearances. The critic Richard Sennett has described a nineteenth-century "doctrine of secular immanence" which presumed that "personality varies among people, and is unstable within each person because appearances have no distance from impulse." Since appearances could be modified at any time, the self became destabilized, with "consciousness always follow[ing] emotional expression in this scheme."[43] Instead of the soul's emotions effecting the facial expression, in other words, it was the facial expression that affected the inner workings of the self.

This view recalls Charles Baudelaire's earlier contention that in acting, one had only to compose one's face in a particular way in order to elicit corresponding sentiments.[44] Duchenne himself conceded that individuals with theatrical abilities could imagine specific emotional states and enact the appropriate expressions:

> It is very true that certain people, comedians above all, possess the art of marvelously feigning emotions that exist only on their faces or lips. In creating an imaginary situation they are able, thanks to a special aptitude, to call up these artificial emotions.[45]

Duchenne had even included an actor of sorts in the "Scientific Section" of *Mécanisme*, where he had his model, "an artist of talent and at the same time an anatomist," "produce perfectly most of the expressions portrayed by each of the muscles of the eyebrow" simply by "calling on his feelings."[46] But his actor/model could produce only "most of the expressions" effected by the eyebrow's muscles; beyond that minimal mimicry, Duchenne was convinced, there were absolute limits to the feigning of emotions. "It will be simple for me," he wrote, "to show that there are some emotions that man cannot simulate or portray artificially on the face; the attentive observer is always able to recognize a false smile."[47] In

FIGURE 38.   Guillaume-Benjamin Duchenne. *Further Aesthetic Electrophysiological Studies* from *Mécanisme de la Physionomie Humaine* (Paris, Veuve Jules Renouard, 1862), fig. 81. Albumen silver print; image: 11.8 x 9.4 cm., volume: 28.6 x 19.2 cm.

both the "Scientific" and the "Aesthetic" sections of *Mécanisme*, Duchenne carefully described how to distinguish between a smile brought about by genuine enjoyment and one occasioned by social politeness: the muscle of the inferior region of the lower eyelid, he noted, "is only brought into play by a genuinely agreeable emotion. Its inertia in [feigned] smiling unmasks a false friend."[48]

Here as elsewhere, Duchenne sought, as far as he was able, photographically to depict the complex, combinatory expressions resulting from often conflicted emotions and ambivalent sentiments, expressions that had already become part of the vocabulary of modern writers and artists. He attempted to articulate visually what historian Barbara Stafford has described as the "amorphous language of the inchoate feelings which exists below the rational articulation of the canonical Cartesian passions."[49] For Duchenne, such expressions could be synthetically manufactured only by electroshock and in the setting of elaborately constructed set pieces featuring gestures and accessory symbols. He thus arranged such melodramatic tableaux as a nun in "extremely sorrowful prayer" experiencing "saintly transports of virginal purity"; a mother feeling both pain and joy while leaning over a child's crib (figure 37); a bare-shouldered coquette looking at once offended, haughty, and mocking; and three scenes of Lady Macbeth expressing the "aggressive and wicked passions, of hatred, of jealousy, of cruel instincts," modulated to varying degrees by contrary feelings of filial piety. Indeed, not only did Duchenne stage specific scenes from *Macbeth*, he also reproduced sections of the play's dialogue in his text so the reader could follow the scenario (figure 38).[50] Elsewhere he prided himself on being able to effect a metamorphosis from the "purest, most angelic smile" into the "most provocative and licentious" smile by simply shocking a single muscle: "I transformed virgins into bacchantes."[51] This theater of pathognomic effects commands most of the "Aesthetic Section" of *Mécanisme*.

AMBIGUOUS MECHANICS

The first paragraph of *Mécanisme* functions as an epigraph of sorts and is drawn from Comte de Buffon's *Histoire de l'homme*, of circa 1749:

> When the spirit is roused, the human face becomes a living picture where the emotions are registered with much delicacy and energy, where each movement of the spirit is expressed by a feature, each action by a characteristic, the swift, sharp impression of which anticipates the will and discloses our most secret feelings.[52]

While Buffon was not completely wedded to a philosophy of Cartesian mechanics,[53] it was precisely a "mechanics of passion" that informed his and nearly all other physiognomic and pathognomic dissertations and their illustrations. For Descartes, the soul was located in the pineal gland, and it was this gland that drove the machine of the body by exciting the neural filaments;[54] for Duchenne, the exact seat of the soul was unimportant, though wherever it lay, it certainly controlled the machine of the body by contracting the facial muscles. If Le Brun's diagrammatic drawings captured and recorded the stormiest of passions in a "pictorial language that was always at the disposal of Reason,"[55] Duchenne's photographs likewise immobilized the "expressive lines and . . . the truth of expression," but in a newer form of pictorial language that was equally at the service of scientific observation.[56] Descartes's bodily mechanics had simply evolved into a mechanical body that could be perceived, measured, and constructed by science.

But eighteenth-century Reason and nineteenth-century Positivism were coming to an end, and in many ways Duchenne represented that conclusion. Duchenne was aware that the viewer's subjectivity often contributed to his or her interpretation of expressions; he himself had fallen into the trap of subjectivity, for instance, by assuming that in expressing pain, the isolated movement of the eyebrow muscle animated the entire face. Much has been made of the startling discovery he made when, early on in his research, he faradically shocked this muscle into contracting at the exact moment when his model's veil accidentally fell over her upper face, drawing attention to the fact that her lower face remained inexpressively neutral throughout the contraction. Duchenne had, indeed, unmasked an "illusion" and a "mirage," but of what consequence was this revelation?[57] Novelists had long recognized the dichotomy, as had most revelers attending masked balls, or any flirtatious ingenue disporting a fan. The Austrian philosopher Ludwig Wittgenstein would later suggest, "Get a human being to give angry, proud, ironical looks; and now veil the face so that only the eyes remain uncovered—in which the whole expression seems concentrated—their expression is now surprisingly *ambiguous*."[58] Looks could deceive, then, and the meaning of an expression be rendered dubious by extraneous accessories such as veils—so much so, indeed, that the German sociologist Georg Simmel could declare in 1901 that "appearance [is] the veiling and unveiling of the soul."[59]

The use-value of facial expressions' signifying precise emotions began to wane in the 1860s. Duranty exhibited a grave mistrust for and cynicism toward such a systematic approach, and Degas tried for a far more relativistic and embracing scheme. In 1865 Pierre Gratiolet, whose book on physiognomics would be included in Chesneau's review, confidently asserted that "there is no movement that does not have its physiognomy," including gestures, postures, and motions of the hands, feet, and limbs.[60] For Chesneau, Gratiolet's book showed "what secret links unite the signs that are spontaneously employed with what is signified, which is to say the idea or sentiments that they manifest . . . directly, sympathetically, symbolically, or metaphorically in external organs."[61] Gratiolet (1815–1865) was a trained physiologist, and his concern for physiognomy was essentially a scientific one—though not entirely so, it would seem, as a physiologist could hardly create objective taxonomies of sympathetic, symbolic, or metaphoric sentiments. Yet these sentiments could be easily rendered by artists, from Degas to Van Gogh and beyond. Antonin Artaud, a French dramatist and artist who was keenly aware of faces, wrote in his essay "Le visage humain" (1947) that Van Gogh "could make of the human head a portrait which was the bursting flare of a throbbing, exploded heart." To this he added, "His own."[62] It was precisely this order of subjectivity in expressing emotions, as well as in reading them, that was lacking not only in Duchenne's but in nearly all other standard theories of physiognomics.

Since mechanical bodies, as well as the observation of them, had by now become infected by the virus of subjectivity, Duchenne's pioneering work may be positioned exactly between Descartes's bodily mechanics and Gilles Deleuze and Félix Guattari's "abstract machine of faciality." Philosopher and psychoanalyst, respectively, the latter propose that the "face is not an envelope exterior to the person who speaks, thinks, or feels," faces do not come "ready-made" but instead are

> engendered by an abstract machine of faciality (*visagéité*), which produces them at the same time as it gives the signifier its white wall and subjectivity its black hole. Thus the black hole/white wall system is, to begin with, not a face but the abstract machine that produces faces according to the changeable combinations of its cogwheels.[63]

Artists since Duchenne's time have continued to portray faces and their expressive countenances, but the human face has for the most part evolved into what critic John Welchman has called a "double zone of distortion and reduction": "No longer a mirror for the soul or an assigned marker for the narrative flows, it has eventually become an arena of *facture* among other adjacent places, other marks."[64] And if the ultimate condition of subjectivity is a "body without organs," one might infer that the face is itself an organ without a body, "alienated from the body and the social envelope alike, or . . . reconvened as a structure, invaded and controlled by the outside."[65]

A THEATER OF THE PASSIONS

Since Duchenne, a decided rupture between the soul and its physiognomic expression has taken place; our vision has shifted, in the words of novelist Kōbō Abe, "from the classical harmony of heart and face to the representation of character devoid of harmony, completely collapsing into Picasso's eight-sided faces and Klee's *False Face*."[66] Cartesian mechanics have become far more fluid, the truth of photography more suspect, the normal and the pathological more alike, and the face and the mask more interchangeable. How, then, may we position Duchenne's *Mécanisme de la physionomie humaine*, this rare and fascinating curiosity of medical literature and art theory? To be sure, in his attempt to visualize the soul's emotions, Duchenne firmly established the modern, biological concept of emotional expression.[67] *Mécanisme* was the first essay on "psycho-physiology" that was truly scientific in its methods. Duchenne's *Mécanisme* has remained the foundation for most of the research that still continues despite his many physiological errors, his myological oversimplifications, his insistence on observational description instead of explanation, his nearly complete lack of interest in the expressive characteristics of the eyes, and his frequent references to God when in doubt. In short, Duchenne created a monument, at once both absurd and revealing, to what Welchman has called the "rationalism of biological (and spiritual) engineering."[68]

Duchenne's most famous student, Jean-Martin Charcot (1825–1893), became director of the Salpêtrière in 1862, adopted Duchenne's photographic experiments, and named an examination room at the asylum after his teacher. Like Duchenne, Charcot sought taxonomically to chart the gestures and expressions of his patients and believed as well that these expressions were subject to laws that governed them with the "regularity of a mechanism."[69] Unlike Duchenne, however, Charcot was interested exclusively in pathological subjects, viewing the population of more than five thousand patients at the Salpêtrière as a "living pathological museum."[70] He encouraged the photographing of hysterics and epileptics by Paul Régnard, as well as Albert Londe's application of chronophotography in recording the writhings of epileptics, hystero-epileptics, and grand hysterics.[71] If Duchenne had felt obliged to pose his female subject like a mannequin, Charcot went so far as to choreograph a troupe of actresses; one colleague described an experiment in which verbal suggestions induced a female patient to hallucinate and perform "like an actor who, beset by madness, imagines that the drama she plays is a reality, not a fiction," assuming and speaking the roles of a peasant, an actress, and a nun in quick succession.[72] Each Tuesday, Charcot also staged what amounted to a "theater of the passions," in which an audience made up of high society and those devoted to scientific reason and medical jurisdiction was confronted by the "uncontrollable fits and rages of hysterical bodies" and by what sociologist John O'Neill has termed the "transgressive possibilities" of an "erotics of a male science imposing itself upon a female body."[73]

Duchenne's ultimate legacy may have consisted in his setting the stage, as it were, for Charcot's visual theater of the passions, and in defining the essential dramaturgy of all the visual theaters, both scientific and artistic, that have since been enacted in attempting to picture our inner psyches. Since the publication of Duchenne's largely forgotten masterpiece of nineteenth-century "scientific" documentation, photography as well as film and video have played an ever-expanding role in subsuming physiognomic studies.[74] There is a kind of Futurist theater of the face, in Anton Bragaglia's chronophotographic *Polyphysionomic Portrait* of 1930, and a Surrealist theater of the emotions in Salvador Dalí's photomontage *The Phenomenon of Ecstasy* of 1933.[75] A psychological theater, too, is surely at work in Diane Arbus's photographs, especially in her final images, and in the still melodramas of Cindy Sherman. The influence of Duchenne's (and Charcot's) dramaturgy may likewise be clearly present in such early popular films as the American Mutoscope and Biograph Company's *Female Facial Expressions* (1902),[76] in Marion Davies's array of expressions in King Vidor's *Show People* (1928), in Richard Widmark's furtive aspect in the opening scene of Samuel Fuller's *Pickup on South Street* (1953), and in Madeline Kahn's swooning in Mel Brooks's *Young Frankenstein* (1974). The list could be extended endlessly and would certainly have to include videos by Bruce Nauman and Douglas Gordon. Suffice it to say that what Le Brun's system was to eighteenth- and nineteenth-century theater and history painting, Duchenne's photography was, at least metaphorically, to twentieth-century photography and film, in their appeal to what Artaud called the "cruelty and terror" that "confront us with all our possibilities."[77] In the end, Duchenne's *Mécanisme de la physionomie humaine* and the photographic stills from its experimental theater of electroshock excitations simply established the modern field on which the struggle to picture and thus discern the ever-elusive meanings of our coded faces continues even now to be waged.[78]

Notes

This essay has evolved into a longer chapter within the author's forthcoming *"Ghost in the Shell" Photography and the Human Soul, 1850–2000*, an exhibition catalogue to be published by the Los Angeles County Museum of Art in late 1999. I would like to thank the Houghton Library and its staff for asking me to write this essay and for stimulating me into finally consolidating more than thirty years of research into the subject of human faciality.

1. "Photography of the Passions," trans. from *L'Ami des sciences*, *The Photographic News* 2, no. 43 (July 1, 1859): 198; a review of a lecture by a Dr. Malley "on an album of the mechanism of the physiognomy, composed by M. Duchenne." Elsewhere, however, we read that this contribution to *L'Ami des sciences*, edited by Victor Meunier, was by a certain Dr. Mallez; see La Gavinie, "Chronique," *La Lumière* 9, no. 9 (February 26, 1859): 36.

2. Dr. G.-B. Duchenne de Boulogne, *Mécanisme de la physionomie humaine, ou Analyse électro-physiologique de l'expression des passions applicable à la pratique des arts plastiques* (Paris: Vᵉ Jules Renouard, 1862). This work has recently been published in English; see G.-B. Duchenne de Boulogne, *The Mechanism of Human Facial Expression*, ed. and trans. R. Andrew Cuthbertson (Cambridge: Cambridge University Press, 1990). Unless otherwise noted, I will cite the first French edition (hereafter "Duchenne, *Mécanisme*") and use Cuthbertson's admirable translation of this work (hereafter "Cuthbertson trans."). The Harrison D. Horblit Collection of Early

Photography at the Houghton Library, Harvard University, contains two copies of the first edition, one with eighty-eight plates of albumen prints, the other with ninety-three. Charles Darwin was wrong when he stated that the work appeared in both folio and octavo editions; of the two copies in the Houghton Library, one, a dedication copy to the physician Aristide Auguste Verneuil (1823–1895), is a large octavo, while the other is quarto in format; cf. Charles Darwin, *The Expression of the Emotions in Man and Animals* (London: John Murray, 1872), 5. Duchenne's publisher announced that a "deluxe," "grand-in-quarto," limited edition of the work was available as a boxed set, though Jean-François Debord of the Ecole Nationale Supérieure des Beaux-Arts doubts if any were actually made; cf. Jean-François Debord, "The Duchenne de Boulogne Collection in the Department of Morphology, L'Ecole Nationale Supérieure des Beaux-Arts," in Cuthbertson trans., 243.

3. For further details of Duchenne's life, see Emanuel B. Kaplan, "Duchenne of Boulogne and the Physiologie des Mouvements," in *Victor Robinson Memorial Volume: Essays on History of Medicine*, ed. Solomon R. Kagan (New York: Froben Press, 1948), 177–92. (Note: the author of this reference to Duchenne is frequently and erroneously cited in the literature as Emanuel Bikaplan [sic].) Also cf. Nancy Ann Roth, "Electrical Expressions: The Photographs of Duchenne de Boulogne," in *Multiple Views: Logan Grant Essays on Photography, 1983–89* (Albuquerque: University of New

Mexico Press, 1991), 105–37; and Tarah Rider, *Dr. Guillaume Benjamin-Armand Duchenne*, History of Photography Monograph Series No. 25 (Tempe: Arizona State University, 1989), unpaginated. The earliest mention of "electropuncture" appears in J. B. Sarlandières, *Mémoires sur l'électro-puncture: considérée comme moyen nouveau de traiter efficacement la goutte, les rhumatismes et les affections nerveuses, et sur l'emploi du moxa japonaia en France* (Paris: Mlle. Delaunay, 1825); cf. R. Andrew Cuthbertson, "The Highly Original Dr. Duchenne," in Cuthbertson trans., 231, n. 36.

4. Electropuncture was invasive insofar as the skin of the patient had to be punctured by sharp electrodes; Duchenne's invention was noninvasive and used an alternating "faradic" current and small moistened electrodes. Cf. Cuthbertson, "The Highly Original Dr. Duchenne," 231.

5. Duchenne, *Mécanisme*, part 3, 141; Cuthbertson trans., 105

6. Duchenne, *Mécanisme*, part 3, 129; Cuthbertson trans., 101.

7. Paul Guilly, *Duchenne de Boulogne* (Paris: J.-B. Baillière et fils, 1936), 196.

8. Duchenne, *Mécanisme*, part 2, v–vi; Cuthbertson trans., 39.

9. The publication of Duchenne's *Mécanisme de la physionomie humaine* by Ve Jules Renouard was far from straightforward: its three fascicles—"Considérations Générales," "Partie Scientifique," and "Partie Esthétique"—did not appear at once, but rather months apart, in two segments. Each of the few complete copies produced had to have an original albumen photograph pasted in as frontispiece and another ninety or so pasted into the "atlas" of plates. The title page in some examples of *Mécanisme* announces "Avec un atlas composé de 74 figures électro-physiologiques photographiées," while others more tersely state "album." Since both copies in the Horblit donation bear the extended announcement, I will refer to the pictorial volume as the "atlas." The "Aesthetic Section," not envisioned at the outset, was an afterthought, as were its additional plates and the nine "tableaux synoptiques" at the end. A complete copy may exist, therefore, in a single volume or as many as four. Text pages are numbered i–viii and 1–70 in the "General Considerations," i–xi and 1–128 in the "Scientific

Section," and 129–94 in the "Aesthetic Section." The photographic plates are similarly confusing. The title page reads "avec un atlas composé de 74 figures photographiés," while the preface to the "Scientific Section" refers to an "album complet se composé de soixante-douze figures photographiés," which claim is true if one counts the frontispiece as part of the plates numbered 3–73; three text engravings are numbered 1, 2, and 2bis. An unspecified number of these photographs were executed in 1854 by the photographer Adrien Tournachon, whom Duchenne credits in the text; see Duchenne, *Mécanisme*, part 2, vi; Cuthbertson trans., 39. The majority of photographs in the "Scientific Section," however, were taken by Duchenne himself as early as 1852, but mostly in 1856. The eleven plates corresponding to the "Aesthetic Section" were taken by Duchenne in 1862, as were the final nine synoptic plates. I am deeply indebted to Richard Yanul, historian of photographically illustrated books, who years ago supplied me with much of the bibliographic information contained in this paragraph (Richard Yanul to Robert Sobieszek, a.l.s., August 29, 1972). It should be noted that while the bibliography in Guilly does not cite a second edition of *Mécanisme*, one was published by J.-B. Ballière in 1876, containing a frontispiece portrait of Duchenne and his elderly male subject and the nine synoptic plates. See auction catalogue *Photographs* Sale LN8302 (London: Sotheby's May 7, 1998), lot 136.

This second edition is also noted in Elisabeth Madlener, "Ein Kabbalistischer Schauplatz: Die physiognomische Seelenerkundung," in Jean Clair, Cathrin Pichler, and Wolfgang Pircher, eds., *Wunderblock: Eine Geschichte der modernen Seele*, exh. cat. (Vienna: Löcker Verlag and Wiener Festwochen, 1989), 179, n. 34.

10. Duchenne, *Mécanisme*, part 1, 53; Cuthbertson trans., 31.

11. Duchenne, *Mécanisme*, part 2, 82; Cuthbertson trans., 81.

12. Duchenne, *Mécanisme*, part 2, 6; Cuthbertson trans., 42. A portrait of Duchenne and this model also appears as the frontispiece to his *Album de photographies pathologiques, complémentaire du livre intitulé De l'électrisation localisée*. Apparently Duchenne took photographs of another male model in similar experiments in 1856–57, but those images, currently in the collection of the

Kunstforum Läderbank in Vienna, were not used in Mécanisme; cf. Madlener, "Ein Kabalistischer Schauplatz," 173–74.

13. Duchenne, *Mécanisme*, part 2, 7; Cuthbertson trans., 43.

14. Duchenne, *Mécanisme*, part 2, 7; Cuthbertson trans., 43. Duchenne's phrase is "saisissantes de vérité."

15. Duchenne, *Mécanisme*, part 3, 130–32; Cuthbertson trans., 101–102.

16. Duchenne, *Mécanisme*, part 3, 133; Cuthbertson trans., 102. Duchenne's phrase is "au point de vue plastique."

17. Duchenne, *Mécanisme*, part 3, 133–35; Cuthbertson trans., 102–103.

18. Duchenne, *Mécanisme*, part 3, 141; Cuthbertson trans., 105.

19. Cf. Jurgis Baltrusaitis, "Animal Physiognomy," in *Aberrations: An Essay on the Legend of Forms*, trans. Richard Miller (Cambridge: The MIT Press, 1989), 5.

20. Cf. Wylie Sypher, "The Late-Baroque Image: Poussin and Racine," *Magazine of Art* 45, no. 5 (May 1952): 209–15; also cf. Janet Browne, "Darwin and the Expression of the Emotions," in *The Darwinian Heritage*, ed. David Kohn (Princeton: Princeton University Press, 1985), 324, n. 8.

21. Cf. Patrizia Magli, "The Face and the Soul," trans. Ughetta Lubin, in *Zone 4: Fragments for a History of the Human Body*, part 2, ed. Michel Feher et al. (New York: Zone Books, 1989), 89–92.

22. Graeme Tytler, *Physiognomy in the European Novel: Faces and Fortunes* (Princeton: Princeton University Press, 1982), 86–90.

23. Ibid., 65.

24. Ibid., 87.

25. Charles Bell, *The Anatomy and Philosophy of Expression as Connected with the Fine Arts*, 7th ed., (London: George Bell and Sons, 1877), 55–56.

26. Duchenne, *Mécanisme*, part 1, 4–5; Cuthbertson trans., 4.

27. Michel Foucault, *The Birth of the Clinic: An Archaeology of Medical Perception*, trans. A. M. Sheridan Smith (New York: Vintage Books, 1975), 198.

28. Darwin, *The Expression of the Emotions in Man and Animals*, 289–300; also cf. Sander L. Gilman, "Darwin Sees the Insane," *Journal of the History of the Behavioral Sciences* 15 (1979), 253–62.

29. Cf. Gilman, "Darwin Sees the Insane," 261.

30. Duchenne, *Mécanisme*, part 2, 8; Cuthbertson trans., 43.

31. Duchenne, *Mécanisme*, part 3, 133; Cuthbertson trans., 102.

32. Duchenne, *Mécanisme*, part 3, 130–31, my translation; cf. Cuthbertson trans., 101, where *moralement* is translated as "spiritually," and *émotions de l'âme* appears as "his or her emotions." Despite an otherwise competent translation of Duchenne's text, Cuthbertson, a physiologist and medical historian, here seems determined to make Duchenne even more clinical than he was or could have been at the time.

33. Duchenne, *Mécanisme*, part 3, n. 152; Cuthbertson trans., n. 110. Photography critic Francis Wey, noting the differences between naturalism and realism in 1851, remarked that the realists "make the maxim 'Nothing is beautiful but truth' prevail in an absolute sense" (Francis Wey, "Du naturalisme dans l'art: de son principe et de ses conséquences," *La Lumière* 1, no. 8 [March 30, 1851]: 31).

34. Duchenne, *Mécanisme*, part 1, 65; Cuthbertson trans., 36.

35. Duchenne, *Mécanisme*, part 2, vi; Cuthbertson trans., 39.

36. Duchenne, *Mécanisme*, part 2, ix; Cuthbertson trans., 40.

37. Duchenne, *Mécanisme*, part 3, 152 n.; Cuthbertson trans., 110 n.

38. Ernest Chesneau, "De la physionomie," part 1, *Le Constitutionnel* 51, no. 282 (October 9, 1866): [1].

39. Edmond Duranty, "Sur la physionomie," *La Revue Libérale* 2 (1867): 510; trans. and quoted in Theodore Reff, Degas: *The Artist's Mind*, exh. cat. (New York: The Metropolitan Museum of Art, 1976), 219. Duranty's essay appeared serially, beginning in the July 25 and ending in the August 25, 1867, issue. See Marcel Crouzet, *Un Méconnu du Réalisme: Duranty (1833–1880), L'Homme, Le Critique, Le Romancier* (Paris: Librairie Nizet, 1964), 248 n. 73.

40. Quoted in Crouzet, *Un Méconnu du Réalisme*, 248. To be accurate, Descartes had said much the same when he declared that passions were easily feigned and often misleading; cf. Tom Gunning, "In Your Face: Physiognomy, Photography, and the Gnostic Mission of Early Film," *Modernism/Modernity* 4, no. 1 (January 1997): 4.

41. While Balzac was dependent upon Lavater for most of his physiognomic beliefs, he was also fairly relativistic. In *Une fille d'Eve*, he declared that previously "the caste system gave each person a physiognomy which was more important than the individual, today the individual gets his physiognomy from himself"; quoted in Judith Wechsler, *A Human Comedy: Physiognomy and Caricature in Nineteenth-Century Paris* (Chicago: University of Chicago Press, 1982), 29.

42. Notebook 23, page 44; quoted in Reff, *Degas: The Artist's Mind*, 217. Duranty had already pointed to the importance of symbolic accessories in discerning character; for him, after Lavater described the "complicated but always open book that is the physiognomy, it seems that people became discouraged and wanted to look for an explanation in accessory signs that no one knew how to decipher." See Duranty, "Sur la physionomie" (July 25, 1867), 506; quoted in Elizabeth Anne McCauley, *A. A. E. Disdéri and the Carte de Visite Portrait Photograph* (New Haven: Yale University Press, 1985), 169.

43. Richard Sennett, *The Fall of Public Man* (New York: Vintage Books, 1978), 150–53.

44. Charles Baudelaire, "Philibert Rouvière," in *Oeuvres complètes*, rev. and ed. Claude Pichois (Paris: Bibliothèque de la pléiade, 1961), 574. Cf. also Jean Pommier, *La Mystique de Baudelaire* (Geneva: Slatkine Reprints, 1967), 48. Earlier, Johann Engel, in his *Ideen zu einer Mimik* (Berlin, 1785), had suggested that outward actions could influence the soul; cf. Barbara Stafford, *Symbol and Myth: Humbert de Superville's Essay on Absolute Signs in Art* (Cranbury, N.J.: University of Delaware Press and Associated University Presses, 1979), 20.

45. Cf. Duchenne, *Mécanisme*, part 1, 51–52; Cuthbertson trans., 30.

46. Plates 4, 15–16, and 23–25. Cf. Duchenne, *Mécanisme*, part 2, 8–9; Cuthbertson trans., 44. It may be noted that Darwin commissioned Swedish-born photographer Oscar Gustave Rejlander to create self-portraits enacting the expressions and gestures of surprise, disgust, helplessness, and indignation. See Darwin, *The Expression of the Emotions in Man and Animals*, 23. Much of the scientific literature of the period, such as Theodor Piderit's *Wissenschaftliches System der Mimik und Physiognomik* (Detmold, 1867), saw no problem in comparing actual expressions of the emotions with emotions that were acted; cf. Tytler, *Physiognomy in the European Novel*, 86–87.

47. Cf. Duchenne, *Mécanisme*, part 1, 51–52; Cuthbertson trans., 30.

48. Cf. Duchenne, *Mécanisme*, part 2, 63, part 3, 188; Cuthbertson trans., 72, 128.

49. Barbara Maria Stafford, "'Peculiar Marks': Lavater and the Countenance of Blemished Thought," *Art Journal* 46, no. 3 (Fall 1987): 186. Stafford is here discussing Georg Christoph Lichtenberg's "semiotics of affects."

50. Cf. Duchenne, *Mécanisme*, part 3, 169–74; Cuthbertson trans., 120–22.

51. Cf. Duchenne, *Mécanisme*, part 3, 151; Cuthbertson trans., 110.

52. Cf. Duchenne, *Mécanisme*, part 1, 5; Cuthbertson trans., 1.

53. Cf. Barbara Maria Stafford, *Body Criticism: Imaging the Unseen in Enlightenment Art and Medicine* (Cambridge: The MIT Press, 1991), 322.

54. Cf. Sypher, "The Late-Baroque Image," 212.

55. Brewster Rogerson, "The Art of Painting the Passions," *Journal of the History of Ideas* 14, no. 1 (January 1953): 76.

56. Cf. Duchenne, *Mécanisme*, part 3, 134; Cuthbertson trans., 103.

57. Cf. Duchenne, *Mécanisme*, part 1, 20; Cuthbertson trans., 13.

58. Ludwig Wittgenstein, *Zettel*, ed. G. E. M. Anscombe and G. H. Wright, trans. G. E. M. Anscombe (Berkeley: University of California Press, 1970), 41e.

59. Georg Simmel, "Aesthetic Significance of the Face," trans. Lore Ferguson, in *Essays on Sociology, Philosophy and Aesthetics*, ed. Kurt H. Wolff (New York: Harper Torchbooks, 1959), 281.

60. Pierre Gratiolet, *De la physionomie et des mouvements d'expression. Suivi d'une notice sur sa vie et ses travaux, et de la nomenclature de ses ouvrages par Louis Grandeau* (Paris: J. Hetzel, 1865); quoted in Ernest Chesneau, "De la physionomie," part 2, *Le Constitutionnel* 51, no. 288 (October 16, 1866): [2].

61. Ibid.

62. Antonin Artaud, "Le visage humain . . . ," in *Antonin Artaud: Works on Paper*, exh. cat., ed. Margit Rowell, trans. Roger McKeon (New York: Museum of Modern Art, 1996), 95.

63. Gilles Deleuze and Félix Guattari, *A Thousand Plateaus: Capitalism & Schizophrenia*, trans. Brian Massumi (Minneapolis: University of Minnesota Press, 1987): 167–68.

64. John Welchman, "Face(t)s: Notes on Faciality," *Artforum* 27, no. 3 (November 1988), 135.

65. Ibid., 131.

66. Kōbō Abe, *The Face of Another*, trans. E. Dale Saunders (Tokyo: Charles E. Tuttle, 1967), 45.

67. Cf. Guilly, *Duchenne de Boulogne*, 214.

68. Welchman, "Face(t)s: Notes on Faciality," 134.

69. Jean-Martin Charcot, *Oeuvres complètes* 3 (Paris: Aux Bureaux du Progrès médical/Lecrosnier & Babé, 1886–93), 15; quoted in Georges Didi-Huberman, *Invention de l'hystérie: Charcot et l'iconographie photographique de la Salpêtrière* (Paris: Macula, 1982), 78.

70. Charcot, "Leçons sur les maladies du système nerveux," *Oeuvres complètes* 3, no. 4; quoted in Didi-Huberman, *Invention de l'hystérie*, 275.

71. Desiré-Magloire Bourneville, "Préface," in Bourneville and Paul Régnard, *L'Iconographie photographique de la Salpêtrière* 1 (Paris: Aux Bureaux du Progrès médical/Delahaye & Lecrosnier, 1876–77): iii–iv; quoted in Didi-Huberman, *Invention de l'hystérie*, 277. Also, Albert Londe, *La Photographie médicale: application aux sciences médicales et physiologiques* (Paris: Gauthier-Villars, 1893), 3–4; quoted in Didi-Huberman, *Invention de l'hystérie*, 279.

72. Paul Richer, *Etudes cliniques sur la grande hystérie ou hystéro-épilepsie*, 2nd ed. (Paris: Delahaye & Lecrosnier, 1881), 728–30; quoted in Didi-Huberman, *Invention de l'hystérie*, 287.

73. John O'Neill, "The Question of an Introduction: Understanding and the Passion of Ignorance," in *Freud and the Passions*, ed. John O'Neill (University Park, Pa.: The Pennsylvania State University Press, 1996), 10.

74. Welchman, "Face(t)s: Notes on Faciality," 136.

75. For Bragaglia, see Giovanni Lista, ed., *Photographie futuriste italienne: 1911–1939*, exh. cat. (Paris: Musée d'Art Moderne de la Ville de Paris, 1981), 43, pl. 30; for Dalí, see Rosalind Krauss and Jane Livingston, *L'Amour fou: Photography and Surrealism*, exh. cat. (New York: Abbeville Press, 1985), 26, fig. 17.

76. This and similar films constitute what film critic Tom Gunning calls a "cinema of attractions," a genre of nonnarrative spectacles sometimes featuring close-ups of faces and grimaces that, according to critic Lisa Cartwright, refuse "self-regulation." See Tom Gunning, "Cinema of Attractions," in Thomas Elsaesser, ed., *Early Cinema: Space, Frame, Narrative* (London: British Film Institute, 1990), 56–62; and Lisa Cartwright, *Screening the Body: Tracing Medicine's Visual Culture* (Minneapolis: University of Minnesota Press, 1995), 16.

77. Antonin Artaud, *The Theater and Its Double*, trans. Mary Caroline Richards (New York: Grove Press, 1958), 86.

78. Cf. Welchman, "Face(t)s: Notes on Faciality," 134.

INDEX

SIX EXPOSURES

Essays in Celebration of the Opening of the

Harrison D. Horblit Collection

of Early Photography

was designed and printed by

Champagne/Lafayette Communications Inc.